Powerful Places
in
Catalonia

Powerful Places in Catalonia

Gary White & Elyn Aviva

Powerful Places in Catalonia

by

Gary White & Elyn Aviva

Copyright © 2010 by Pilgrims Process, Inc.

All rights reserved. No part of this publication, including illustrations, may be reproduced in any form or by any means, electronic or mechanical, including photocopy, recording, or any information storage and retrieval system, without permission in writing from the publisher.

The authors and publisher have made every effort to ensure the accuracy of the information in this book at the time of publication. However, they can not accept any responsibility for any loss, injury, or inconvenience resulting from the use of information contained in this book.

ISBN: 978-0-9826233-1-2

Library of Congress Control Number:

2010921103

Set in Adobe Caslon Pro 11 pt. and Briso Pro 11 pt., with display in Adobe Caslon Pro in various sizes. Cover and title set in Reliq Std and Briso Pro

Cover photo: the Call, Girona, by Elyn Aviva

Contents

Acknowledgments vi

Introduction 1

Exploring Catalunya 6

Experiencing a Powerful Place 9

Barcelona, Barcelonès 12

Nuestra Señora del Vinyet (Sanctuari de la Mare de Déu del Vinyet), Sitges, Garraf 24

Monestir de Montserrat 30

Dolmen de la Cova d'en Daina, Romanyà de la Sélva, Baix Empordà 40

Girona, Gironès 46

La Garrotxa, Garrotxa 58

Sant Joan de les Abadesses, Ripollès 68

Vall de Núria, Ripollès 74

Besalú, Garrotxa 82

Dolmen Puig de Caneres, Darnius, Alt Empordà 90

Cap de Creus, Alt Empordà 98

Afterword 110

Glossary 111

Bibliography 116

Acknowledgments

Gratitude to our mentors and teachers, including Ferran Blasco, Mara Freeman, Juan Li, Sig Lonegren, Anne Parker, R. J. Stewart, and Dominique Susani. Gratitude to all the earth-mystery writers and researchers, including Paul Devereux and Nigel Pennick, who have opened the way for so many others. Gratitude to each other for patience, tolerance, enthusiasm, and inspiration. Gratitude to the land, the stones, the trees, the temples. For those interested in following up with our teachers we offer the following websites:

Ferran Blasco: http://www.zahoriart.com/

Mara Freeman: http://www.chalicecentre.net/

Juan Li: http://www.ichingdao.org/tao/en/biography-of-juan-li.html

Sig Lonegren: http://www.geomancy.org/

Anne Parker: http://latitudewithattitude.com/

R. J. Stewart: http://www.rjstewart.org/

Dominique Susani: http://sacredgeometryarts.com/

Introduction

Over the years we have traveled to a number of unusual places, drawn by curiosity, lured by possibility. Gradually we realized that although many of these sites were interesting, some of them were really powerful. These were places where we felt something out of the ordinary—ranging from a shiver up the spine to an unexpected sense of serenity to a strong intimation that we had entered a "thin place" where the veil between this world and the "other realm" was more easily parted.

What we experienced in these places was an interaction between the energy of the place itself, the human activities at that location (offerings, ceremonies, constructions such as stone circles or temples), and our own openness to experience what was happening at that moment. The feeling that a particular place is powerful can take many forms, and it can be subtle or very strong.

In this guidebook we describe some of the more powerful places we have found in Catalonia and invite you to experience them for yourself. We make no claims as to what you may or may not feel when visiting these sites. We have observed that one person may bask in the energy of a particular site, another may feel nothing at all, and a third may want to leave as quickly as possible.

On one visit inside a large, earth-covered passage grave in Ireland, Elyn felt increasingly uncomfortable and shaky but (against her better judgment) stayed to listen to our guide. Afterwards, Elyn took a survey and discovered that several people had left immediately because they felt so ill at ease—and others thought the cairn was a wonderful place in which to meditate. In an isolated monastery in the mountains of Spain, Elyn and Gary were shown into an abandoned chapel. Instantly, they both felt an incredibly unconditional loving presence. Their companion (a very sensitive and intuitive lady) looked at them in puzzlement. She thought the energy in the room was nothing special.

Sometimes our experience has differed on subsequent visits to the same site. We speculate why this may be, but we realize that experiences can never be repeated—whether it's your first taste of a chocolate gelato cone on a sunny day in Rome, or your first kiss, or your first visit to the Grand Canyon. As the Greek philosopher Heraclitus said, "No man ever steps in the same river twice, for it's not the same river and he's not the same man." This is equally true of powerful places.

What makes a place powerful?

The brief answer to "what" is: the land itself has underground water lines, faults or cracks in the earth (sometimes called fire lines), energy vortices, "blind" springs, and so on that our ancestors were able to sense and utilize. An old Gaulish word, *wouivre*, refers to snakes that glide, to rivers that snake through the landscape, and to telluric currents that snake underground from the depths of the terrestrial strata. Experienced dowsers using dowsing rods or pendulums can locate these underground features with great accuracy. If they couldn't, oil exploration and well-digging companies wouldn't waste their money on hiring them.

Our ancestors utilized these energies—and their knowledge of geometry (circles, triangles, pyramid shapes, etc.)—to construct sacred places. For example, an alignment of standing stones may have been placed to draw off energy from an underground fault; a circle of stones may have been built to utilize the energy of an underground spring. The altar of a twelfth-century church may have been carefully placed over the crossing of underground water and fire lines.

How do you sense these energies?

The brief answer to how to sense these energies is: by centering, grounding, and being present to a site *in whatever way works for you.* Feeling the subtle energies that are present in a place requires sensitivity and intuition. It is a bit like tuning a radio dial to a particular frequency. These techniques can be taught (we have studied with several teachers who have taught us how). Such instruction is outside the scope of this guidebook, although we do give a few suggestions for how you can be more attuned to a powerful place.

We encourage you to listen carefully to your own inner guidance as you open yourself to what may be available to you at a particular place on a particular day, at a particular time of day, with the particular predisposition you bring at that moment. You must use your own judgment about what is good or not good for you. Trust your feelings—and enjoy the mystery.

A few more things to notice

Ancient people often constructed several sites at some distance from each other. These sites often appear to have a visual (and probably energetic) relationship to each other and to prominent natural features such as hilltops, gaps between hills, etc. This phenomenon is called "intervisibility" and the landscapes themselves are called ritual landscapes. In other words, a powerful place should be experienced in relationship to its surroundings. Prominent ritual landscapes occur in the areas around the Calanais Stones in Scotland; the alignments at Carnac in Brittany, France; various sites in County Sligo, Ireland; the Nosterfield area in England; and Stonehenge in Wiltshire, England, among others. There is much speculation about the purpose of these landscapes, but it is increasingly clear that they exist and were created intentionally.

Not only were sacred sites constructed with an awareness of the energies of the earth and in relationship to each other and to surrounding natural features—they were also often built to interact with solar, lunar, or stellar events. For example, the light of the setting winter solstice sun shines into the entry passageway of Maeshowe, a site described in *Powerful Places in Scotland.* Just as churches used to be constructed so that the altar was in the east (facing the rising sun and signifying the resurrected Christ), so were many megalithic sites designed to take advantage of recurring seasonal astronomical events. Unfortunately, it is often difficult to prove which, or how many, events were being marked.

Organization

Each chapter begins with a brief account by Elyn of a visit to a particular powerful place. This is followed by information about the site along with suggestions, quotations, and related graphics. At the end of each chapter are directions on how to get there and a brief space (Notes) for you to add your own observations. The guidebook concludes with a glossary and bibliography.

How did we choose these particular locations? We talked with people; we did research in books and on the web to discover possible powerful places that were not likely to be on every tourist's itinerary; we visited Catalonia on several occasions with guides and without; and we paid attention to what we experienced at different sites. We then selected powerful places to include in this guidebook.

This specialized guidebook is not an exhaustive listing of all the powerful places in Catalonia; to do that would require a much larger book. Nor is it a complete guide to what to see or where to stay in northeastern Spain. For that you'll need to consult a general travel book. This guidebook *is* intended as an invitation to experience powerful places in Catalonia. We hope that it's the beginning of a conversation. We'd like to hear from you.

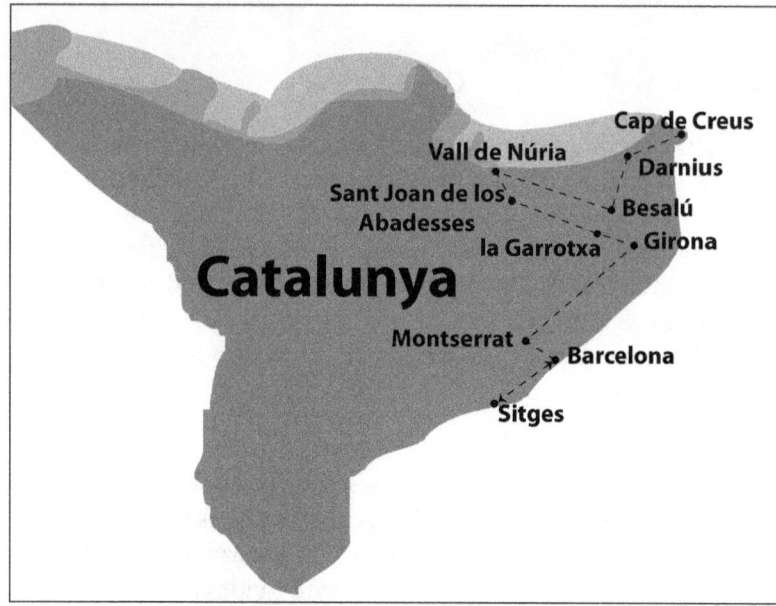

Exploring Catalunya

The map above presents one possible itinerary around Catalonia. The route can easily be negotiated by automobile, but it is only one approach to the region. Most people will arrive in Barcelona, so our itinerary begins there.

Catalunya is the Catalan spelling of Catalonia, and from now on we will use Catalan spelling for locations. (We also provide English and occasionally Spanish place names.) Spain is a country with various dialects and several regional languages. In Catalunya they speak Catalan, a Romance language closely related to Provençal or Occitan, the medieval languages of southern France. It's not a dialect of Spanish; it's a different language. But don't worry: Catalunya is officially bilingual (Catalan/Spanish). If you speak Spanish, French, or English, you can manage to read

A human tower

the signs and make yourself understood. Catalans are used to foreigners, and most people speak Spanish or English in addition to Catalan.

Catalunya: a once-independent, sea-going nation that has been politically tethered to Spain. Known for its *castells* (human towers), sometimes eight or nine tiers high, bonfires at the Summer Solstice, *sardana* folk dance, "Barça" soccer team, cosmopolitan capital—Barcelona, and tremendous pride, Catalunya was an independent entity over 1,000 years ago—and has had its own government, the Generalitat, for 650. It is a land of great physical beauty, stretching from the rugged Pyrenees in the north to the beautiful Costa Brava on the east. It has something (or a lot) for everyone: wonderful natural parks; 5,000-year-old megaliths; Iberian, Greek, and Roman ruins; important medieval monuments; stunning *modernista* architecture by Gaudí and compatriots—not to mention museums dedicated to Dalí (a native son) and Picasso (an honorary Catalan).

Catalunya has always been a bit "testy." The medieval Catalan oath of allegiance to the king was, "We who are as good as you swear to you who are no better than we, to accept you as our king and sovereign lord, provided you observe all our liberties and laws; but if not, not." Home to a fervent nationalist movement, it declared itself an independent republic in 1931—which was rejected by Spain. Catalunya was the Republicans' chief stronghold at the end of the Civil War, and it paid heavily for its temerity under the dictatorship of Franco. He prohibited the public use of Catalan and the *sardana* circle dance, hoping to destroy the Catalan spirit. He failed. Times have changed, and today Catalans swing an inordinate amount of weight in the Spanish parliament, where they wheel and deal from a position of great self-confidence.

Experiencing a Powerful Place

This is a guidebook about *experiencing* places—not just seeing them. You may have already developed your own way to visit a powerful place. If not, the following may be of use.

Much of the time we humans operate on "automatic," hardly registering where we are or what we feel. Visiting a powerful place is an opportunity to be intentional and alert. In order to fully experience a powerful place, it is important to be present. Really conscious. Really aware of your surroundings and of changes in yourself in response to your surroundings. We suggest an acronym, **BLESSING**, to help remember how to prepare to enter a powerful place—whether it is a forest, a church, or a stone circle.

> Going to a powerful place is like getting to know a new friend. Don't rush in. Say "hello." Introduce yourself. Bring a "hostess" gift. Listen politely to what the site has to tell you. Don't be rude or impatient. Don't interrupt. Have a conversation. When you (and it) are finished, don't just leave—remember to say goodbye. And realize that not every powerful place wants to be befriended! Some might be positively taciturn or even grumpy.

BLESSING stands for: **B**reathe slowly and regularly, paying attention to your breath moving in and out. If you have a breathing practice, now is the time to do it. **L**ook and **L**isten within: what are you sensing internally? How do you feel? **E**stablish yourself in your location, perhaps by orienting to the seven directions (east, south, west, north, above, below, and the center within—or, before you, behind you, to your right, to your left, above, below, and the center within). **S**ense your surroundings, opening up your five senses (and sixth sense) to what is around you. State your **IN**tention to respect this place, to experience what is present. **G**ive gratitude for this opportunity.

> In approaching a powerful place, it is very important that we prepare ourselves mentally, emotionally, psychologically, and physically for the experience because what we feel is very much determined by what we bring to the site. Purposeful preparation becomes the prerequisite for having meaningful experiences.

One of our mentors, Mara Freeman, suggests the acronym **ECOLOGY** for remembering how to approach a stone circle. It can, of course, be modified to apply to powerful places in general. "E" stands for **E**ntry, which means enter by first circling the site in a clockwise (sunwise) direction. "C" is for **C**entering yourself. This is often best accomplished by touching one of the stones. "O" stands for **O**ffering, which can be a bit of grain, milk, a strand of hair, saliva, etc., which shows that you come in good faith. The best offerings are biodegradable so they don't linger in the environment to build up over time. "L" is for **L**istening—listen to the sounds around you: birds, wind, wild creatures, and other sounds of nature. "O" stands for **O**pening up your inner and outer senses. "G" is for **G**ratitude to the place, the Earth, all of life, and Nature. "Y" is for **Y**ou: you should leave a place just as you found it. Take nothing and leave nothing. You can see the result of people not observing this injunction at many popular sacred sites: trees damaged by people taking pieces of their bark or carving on them; sites littered with paper wrappers and trash; melted wax dripped over ancient stones. Observe **ECOLOGY**: the Earth and future visitors will thank you.

La Sagrada Familia

Barcelona, Barcelonès

I'm not a fan of metropoli, but Barcelona has won me over. Great metro system, extensive tourist buses, numerous walking routes from city to sea—there's something for everyone, including me. The Barri Gòtic (Gothic Quarter), with its narrow alleys and ancient buildings leaning towards each other; the cathedral cloister with its flock of thirteen (note that number) geese; the astounding parabolic geometry of Gaudí's La Sagrada Familia, a cathedral for our times, still incomplete after a century; the deeply moving Santa María del Mar, built stone by stone by the faithful; numerous museums (especially the National Museum of Catalan Art, which holds the world's best collection of medieval church murals); the abundant parks; the numerous churches; the moderniste *architecture.... On the Night of St. Joan (the Eve of St. John the Baptist), Barcelonans light bonfires on the beach and burn up their cares and disappointments (and old furniture) or plight their troth, jumping hand in hand over the flames.... Pagan practices are alive and well, along with Catalan pride. What's not to like? (Elyn)*

Barcelona is the most cosmopolitan city in Spain. The art and architecture alone (think Gaudí and Picasso) would attract an international following. Barcelona looks out to the world rather than back to Spain. One hears a melange of many languages on the street, but native Catalan predominates. Yes, Barcelona has a reputation for pickpockets and petty street crime, but hide your valuables and don't carry a bag that can easily be snatched and you should have a good time in the city.

We have chosen four powerful places that you might otherwise miss when you visit Barcelona. These places are somewhat off the beaten path and offer rich experiences for travelers with a spiritual bent.

The Call

We begin in the old town (Barri Gòtic) between the lively Rambla and the Town Hall (Ajuntament). Walk down Carrer de Ferran from the Rambla toward the Plaça Sant Jaume, named after St. James the Greater. After a few blocks you will begin to see on your left small side streets with names like Carrer de l'Arc Sant Ramon del Call and Carrer St. Domènec del Call. Turn in on St. Domènec and you will find yourself in the evocative ancient Jewish quarter of Barcelona—"The Call" (CAHee), the Catalan spelling of a Hebrew word *qahál*, meaning a communal meeting or gathering.

A street in the Call

There is evidence of Jewish presence in Barcelona from the seventh century. From the eleventh century through the thirteenth century, Jews dominated the

Plaque in the Call

commercial and cultural life of the city. There were four synagogues, a rabbinical academy, numerous shops, and a cemetery (perhaps Montjuïc) just outside of town. However, there was systematic anti-Semitism and in 1243 a Jewish ghetto was created to protect the Jews (it was said) from violence. As in other European cities this concentrated the Jewish population into a small area—providing a convenient focus for persecution. On August 5, 1391, the feast day of Santo Domingo, the Call was attacked and the Jewish population slaughtered or ejected. The Escola Mayor Street was renamed Sant Domènec and the main synagogue and most other Jewish property passed into the hands of the King Juan I de Aragón. Today the Jewish origins of the Call are remembered with plaques on several street corners that graphically describe the historic boundaries.

If you walk to Carrer de Marlet, 5, you can enter

The Main Synagogue

what remains of the Sinagoga Mayor—the oldest synagogue in Europe, possibly founded in the fifth century. This small two-room, subterranean space has been recently excavated and is maintained as a museum by a local group (Associació Call de Barcelona). All of the ritual furnishings have been donated. A helpful guide will give you a brief lecture. There is a fee for entrance.

Commemorative wall plaque

Just down the street from the synagogue is a commemorative wall plaque in Hebrew that reads "Holy Foundation of Rabbi Samuel Hassardi, for whom life never ends." The plaque is a replica of the original and has been subjected to defacement by anti-Semitic groups, as you can see in the photo. Today some 1,000 Jewish families live in Barcelona, and two new synagogues meet their religious needs.

As you walk through the narrow, claustrophobic streets of the former Call—the tall buildings blocking out the sun—you can get a faint sense

Façade of Church of Sant Jaume

of what it might have been like in the Middle Ages. Imagine the densely populated medieval Call, its vibrant religious and commercial life contrasting starkly with the constant state of imminent persecution.

When you return to Calle de Ferran stop in the small Church of Sant Jaume (St. James the Greater) on the other side of the street. Over the doorway you can see St. James slaughtering the Moors (Santiago Matamoros). Notice the Star of David (or Seal of Solomon?) and the pilgrim's hat, gourd, and staff carved high over the door. The inside of the church carries on this symbolism and is quite beautiful.

Cathedral Cloister

The cathedral (Catedral de la Santa Creu i Santa Eulàlia) is one of the primary tourist destinations in Barcelona. If you go there, don't miss visiting a place that is much less known—the cathedral cloister. Walk along Calle de Ferran to Plaça Sant Jaume and turn up Calle de Sant Honorat, which runs alongside the Palau de la Generalitat. At the end of the street turn right on Calle de Sant Sever. The entrance to the cloister is just ahead. There is an entry fee.

The first thing you are likely to notice upon entering the cathedral cloister, which dates from 1380-1451, are the thirteen live geese in the interior courtyard. We were told that they stand for Santa Eulàlia, who was martyred when she

Geese in the cloister of the cathedral

was thirteen years old on February 12, 303. It is also said that her Roman captors tortured her thirteen times before decapitating her. The cathedral is dedicated to her and her remains are in the crypt. The official explanation for the geese in the cloister is that geese guarded the cathedral and its treasures in the Middle Ages, but that explanation sounds a bit flighty to us. We have other ideas about the significance of the number thirteen and the symbolic significance of geese— including thirteen lunar months in one year, and the goose as a vehicle connecting earth and the heavens, thus symbolizing spiritual movement. To the Druids, the goose foot was as sign of the solstices and equinoxes.

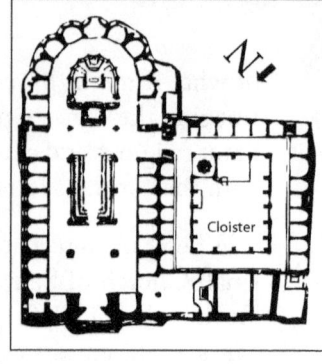

Floor plan of the cathedral

"Since the time of the Romans, the goose has been a symbol of providence and vigilance. The legend of the Capitoline geese that saved Rome from the invasion of the Gauls is well known." George Ferguson. *Signs & Symbols in Christian Art.* London: Oxford University Press, Paperback Edition, 1961, p. 19.

"It is somewhat surprising to see that medieval Christian theology has much less to say about the negative aspects of 13, outside the context of the 12 apostles and the "transgression" of this sacred number. More frequently, 13 was interpreted as a combination of 10 (the Commandments) and the 3 of the Trinity, or, with a different logic, as a combination of the Pentateuch (5) with the Resurrection of Christ (8). It thus was thought to point to the relation between the Old and the New Testaments, which was supposed to become manifest through a combination of work and faith." Annemarie Schimmel. *The Mystery of Numbers.* New York: Oxford University Press, 1993, p. 207.

Located around the cloister are a number of chapels dedicated to various saints. In particular, take notice of the chapel of San Antonio Abad (251–356 CE) who is shown with a pig. We have seen similar statues in other churches (including Santa María del Mar). San Antonio Abad is the patron saint of animals (particularly farm animals) and his saint's day on January 17 is the occasion for a blessing of animals in many parts of the world. It's worth noting that the pig was a sacred animal for the Celts. Perhaps this hints at Celtic connections. He also holds an unusual Tau-topped staff—the staff of "the initiate."

Iglesia Santa Ana

The Church of Santa Ana, which dates from the eleventh century, was originally part of a monastery complex. It mixes Romanesque and Gothic styles in a harmonious blend. The church is hidden away in the northern part of the old city center.

Entrance to Plaça de Ramon Amadeu

Go to the Plaça de Catalunya (easily reached on the metro) and walk down the Rambla de Canaletes. On your left you will see Carrer de Santa Anna. Walk down this street to number 32 on the left. There you will see an archway to Plaça de Ramon Amadeu. Inside this plaza you will see flower sellers and the Church of Santa Ana. Because it is so well hidden the church is rarely visited by tourists.

Saint Ann with Virgin and child

The Church of Santa Ana is dedicated to Saint Ann, the mother of the Virgin Mary. It is oriented with the altar facing east-northeast. We dowsed a wide water line that runs the length of the nave. Behind the central altar is a beautiful bronze statue of St. Ann watching over Mary, who is holding the baby Jesus. They are sheltered under an elaborate baldachin covered with gold leaf and artwork. We sensed a beautiful sweet energy in this church. Take time to be present to the statue of (grand) mother, mother, and child, which seems to radiate unconditional maternal love.

The well in the cloister

In one side chapel you will find a replica of Our Lady of Montserrat (see p. 32), and interesting altar paintings fill other chapels. At the back of the sanctuary is the entrance to the cloister. This is an inner sanctum hidden within this inner sanctum. In the central courtyard is a holy well surrounded by a dense growth of towering trees. The cloister is simple and encourages a contemplative mood. It is a place to spend some time in meditation.

Santa María del Mar

Façade of Santa María del Mar

A much more public place of worship is Santa María del Mar, in the Born district, not far from the popular Picasso Museum. Take the metro to Jaume I and walk down the Carrer de l'Argenteria. Soon you will see the Gothic façade of the church directly ahead. The present building was built in the fourteenth century, largely by volunteer labor from the guild of porters who unloaded ships in the harbor, although the earliest mention of the "church by the sea" dates back to 998 and excavations have revealed a Roman cemetery beneath the current crypt. The main doors (facing south-southwest) show two porters carrying stones on their backs from the quarry in Montjuïc. The story is that King Alfons the Kind donated the stone to build the church with the proviso that the people would have to get the stone to the church themselves. If you want to read a wonderful novel about the

The nave of Santa María del Mar

building of this church, we highly recommend *Cathedral of the Sea* by Ildefonso Falcones. Reading this novel impacted our visit to the church.

Porters carrying cut stones on the main doors

Inside the church, which is usually crowded with visitors (and on Saturdays with wedding parties), you will be struck by its height and spaciousness. The slender octagonal columns are without decoration until near the point where they branch into Gothic arches, which enhances the impression of height. Stained glass windows light up the interior. The central altar, located in the north-northeast, contains a statue of the Virgin that was once over an exterior door. The original Baroque altar and many other images (including the original virgin) were destroyed in a fire during the 1936-39 Civil War. Although some evidence of the fire remains in darkened stone work, the lasting impact was to unclutter the walls and enhance the openness of the space.

Santa María del Mar is noted for its perfect proportions and this, no doubt, is responsible for the harmoniousness of the interior of the church. The proportions may also have something to do with the nearly per-

Ceiling of the crypt in Santa María del Mar

fect acoustics. We were there during a rehearsal for an upcoming wedding and can attest to the exquisite quality of sound in the church.

You may be able to convince the custodian (seated at the desk in the ambulatory behind the altar) to open the crypt for you. You won't see Roman remains, but you will see the reliquary of Sant Cugat. It's a lovely, peaceful spot in which to meditate.

Getting There

You have a number of choices for getting to Barcelona. You can arrive by air, train, boat, or bus. The Barcelona metro system is an excellent way to get around the city and numerous busses go where the metro doesn't. There are several "hop on hop off" tourist busses with recorded guides in several languages that will give you a quick overview of the major areas of the city. Once you are oriented you can use the public transportation or walk through most of the central city. We've intentionally ignored the more popular tourist sights, of which there are many! (http://www.aboutbarcelona.com/ http://www.barcelona-tourist-guide.com/)

Notes

Our Lady of the Vineyard

Nuestra Señora del Vinyet (Sanctuari de la Mare de Déu del Vinyet), Sitges, Garraf

It didn't look like much, this church of Our Lady of the Vineyard, but the custodians lived next door and were quite welcoming. We entered from their home through a low interior doorway into a baroquely decorated temple filled with larger than life-size statues of angels and saints, oil paintings, crystal chandeliers, and an ornately painted, vaulted ceiling. Looking down at us from high above the altar, unfazed by all the hoopla, is the brightly lit focus of attention: the Black Virgin of Vinyet, showcased on a turnstile in the elaborately carved, gilded altarpiece.

Plaque above the side entrance to the sanctuary

We climbed a staircase to her private chamber and turned her 'round. She is tiny, chocolate-colored, and polished smooth, carved from a single piece of wood. The diminutive figure sits on a throne on top of a hidden base, surrounded (and made larger) by a pink, gold-embroidered cape. Over her head is suspended a golden crown and, over that, a pink, gold-embroidered canopy. Angels support the fanciful confection.

I suppressed a smile: the whole thing was a bit over-the-top. But suddenly everything became quite still, and I felt filled with bliss and deep, abiding peace. Unexpectedly, unrequested, I had received her blessing. (Elyn)

The Sanctuary of the Mother of God in Vinyet (Sanctuari de la Mare de Déu del Vinyet) is located on the site of an ancient Roman villa in the outskirts of the town of Sitges. A hermitage has stood on this site from the twelfth century, but it has been rebuilt a number of times. The current building is from the eighteenth century. Some of the furnishings were destroyed in the 1936-37 Civil War. Faithful devotees buried the image of the Black Virgin to protect it, but when it was dug up in 1939 the wood had deteriorated beyond repair. A new figure was commissioned from a local sculptor, Pere Jou. It is a fair replica of the original.

Original Black Virgin figure

Sitges is located on the coast, and for centuries Our Lady has been the object of maritime devotion. Numerous ship *ex votos* used to adorn the sanctuary.

The church is filled with much suggestive symbolism, the origins of which we could not determine, but some of

Checkerboard floor

Our Lady seen from the back in her upstairs chamber

which might be Masonic. These include black and white checkerboard floors, the winged hat of Hermes and the trident carved over the doorway to the right of the altar, and the matching trident on the base of the stand of the Black Virgin—among others. As befits a sanctuary to Our Lady, there is a wealth of Marian imagery, including a painting of Mary, Star of the Sea; Mary being crowned in the painting on the dome at the crossing, in which she is surrounded by stars and a crescent moon lies at her feet; and a painting of Mary of the Morning Star. The references to stars and sea evoke Mary's origins as an ancient goddess, associated with Venus and Isis. And let's not forget that Our Lady of the Vineyard is a Black Virgin. (Also see Montserrat, p. 30.)

"For those who are able to make a leap of faith, our Black Virgin in the west has much in common symbolically with the other great goddess figures of the world. In her subterranean darkness she could be compared with the terrifying maw of death, Kali.... She is also the ancient wisdom of Isis-Maat, the secret of eternal life that is the gold at the end of the alchemical process, as well as the initial blackness. In short, she is the spirit of evolutionary consciousness that lies hidden in matter." Ean Begg. *The Cult of the Black Virgin*. Revised and expanded edition. London: Penguin Books, 1985, p. 131.

Although the sanctuary has been rebuilt numerous times and the current Black Virgin is modern, the Sanctuary of the Mother of God is a very powerful place. When one stands in front of the Black Virgin, the energy is almost palpable. One friend reported feeling almost knocked over from the energy: Elyn, on the other hand, felt that she received a blessing.

Other Things to Do and See

Sitges is a charming, cosmopolitan seaside resort with sixteen beaches, three museums, and several interesting monuments. It has been Barcelona's favorite resort town since the nineteenth century. There are excellent hotels and restaurants along the coast and three ports for boats. Expect all the advantages of a

Area map

popular tourist town as well as all the disadvantages. (http://www.virtourist.com/europe/sitges/Sitges_Spain.htm)

Getting There

Sitges can be reached from Barcelona by bus and train service or by car. Those traveling by boat can put in at one of the ports.

Notes

Montserrat in morning fog

Monestir de Montserrat

It rises suddenly out of the plains, shocking and jagged like a sharp-toothed saw blade: Montserrat. Serrated mountain. Home of La Moreneta, the Black Virgin of Montserrat, celebrated patroness of Catalunya and of the hearts of Catalans.

The road to her sanctuary twists and climbs tortuously up the side of the mountain. We arrive at last, park the car, and follow the trail that winds across the mountain to the Holy Cave. Here, we are told, the statue of the Black Virgin was purportedly found nearly 1000 years ago—or maybe 800 years ago. The plot thickens: perhaps there was a shrine to Venus here, millennia before? The scent of incense suddenly fills the air—I look around, seeking the source. Is the Goddess making herself known?

The next morning we enter the basilica at sunrise, hoping to see La Moreneta up close before the hoards of eager visitors ar-

La Moreneta

rive. We hurry up the flight of stairs to her glittering, mosaic-lined cubicle high above the altar. A miracle occurs: we commune with her undisturbed for half an hour while the monks chant Lauds.

Artist's conception of Montserrat

The sweet sounds waft up from the nave below. I see a gentle smile come and go on La Moreneta's serene face. (Elyn)

Legends abound about Our Lady of Montserrat. According to official church sources a figure known as "La Jerosolimitana" (the native of Jerusalem) was carved in the early days of the Church and brought to Spain by St. Etereo, Bishop of Barcelona. In the seventh century the figure is said to have been hidden from invading Saracens in a cave on the mountain of Montserrat. Then in 890 shepherds heard singing and saw lights on the mountain and rediscovered her. It is likely, however, that the figure we see in the basilica was carved later, in the twelfth or thirteenth century. This figure may have replaced an earlier one, but there is no proof of this. In 1881 Pope Leo XIII proclaimed Our Lady of

1931 postage stamp commemorating La Moreneta

A pilgrim touching Our Lady's globe in the chapel

Montserrat the Patron Saint of Catalunya.

In 1221 King Alfonso X (the Wise) described miracles attributed to Our Lady of Montserrat in his *Canticles*, and the monastery quickly became a major pilgrimage destination. This popularity has continued to the present, with sporadic interruptions caused by wars and other political upheavals. While the number of visitors to the mountain cannot be accurately calculated, it is estimated to be in excess of two million per year. Many people in Catalunya make an annual visit to Montserrat, and many Catalan cultural events are held there. You may be treated to a wedding, a local festival with circles of Catalans dancing the *sardana*, or groups of men climbing on top of each other to create the *castells*, the human towers that are famous throughout Catalunya.

Our Lady of Montserrat is a Black Madonna, one of many such figures found throughout Europe and the Western world. Why is La Moreneta black? There are many conflicting answers to this question. The official Catholic Church view is summarized as follows: "Blackened by candles that burned before the statue day and night, this particular image dates back to at least the twelfth century" (from www.Catholic Tradition.org). Others state that these figures are black because they are carved from dark wood. Some quote the scripture verse, "I am black but comely, O daughters of Jerusalem, . . ." (Song of Songs 1:5) as the basis for the black color. Others say they are dark because Mary fled into Egypt and got sunburned.

Scholars of comparative religion point to the similarity of Black Virgins to statues of Isis and Horus, in which Isis is seated on a throne, facing forward, and the child, Horus, is seated on her lap also facing forward. Some say that the original Isis figures may have been brought back to Europe during the Crusades and morphed into Black Virgins; later Black Madonnas were based on these prototypes. Whatever you choose to believe about Black Madonnas, they have been the subject of considerable interest in the past decades, and often tend to be associated with miracles and healing.

"Every archetype has its seasons. They come and go according to the deepest, often unconscious, needs of the psyche, both personal and collective. Today the Black Madonna is returning. She is coming, not going, and She is calling us to something new (and very ancient, as well). The last time the Black Madonna played a major role in Western culture and psyche was the 12th-century renaissance, a renaissance that the great historian M. D. Chenu said was the 'only renaissance that worked in the West.' It worked because it was grassroots. And from this renaissance was birthed the university, the cathedral, the city itself." Matthew Fox "The Return of the Black Madonna: A Sign of Our Times or How the Black Madonna is Shaking Us Up for the 21st Century." In *The Moonlit Path: Reflections on the Dark Feminine*. Berwick, ME: Nicolas-Hays, Inc., 2003, p. 81.

Visiting Our Lady

La Moreneta resides in an upstairs chapel above the altar in the east end of the church. If you stand in the nave, you can see her inside an open niche high up in the elaborate retablo. Her chapel is reached through a door to the right of the main entrance to the basilica. During the day there are usually long lines of people waiting patiently to spend a few moments in her presence. However, the door to the chapel opens at around 7:00 or 7:30 AM, well before the tourist busses arrive. We stayed overnight and were able to visit her for an extended period of time. This was an amazing opportunity, one that is permanently inscribed in our list of powerful experiences.

View of the nave from the chapel of our Lady

Other Things to Do

The monastery of Montserrat is a very important center of Catalan culture. The museum has an impressive collection of paintings by Catalan artists and old masters. The interactive exhibition called "Montserrat Portes Endins" portrays the life of the Benedictine community at Montserrat. The Montserrat Escolania (boys' choir) is world-famous for the quality of its singing. You can usually hear the choir at mid-day in the basilica. The Montserrat library houses over 300,000 volumes, including rare manuscripts and other unique documents, some of which can be viewed.

Plaza, Montserrat

Chapel at the holy cave of Our Lady of Montserrat

If you enjoy walking, the area has numerous trails that range from easy to quite strenuous, including the Camí de Sant Jaume—the Camino de Santiago! Some trails lead to ancient ruined hermitages scattered on the mountainside. For a different slant on the monastery of Montserrat, consult our book *Powerful Places on the Caminos de Santiago;* you will find additional suggestions for your visit.

Getting There

Hourly trains from Barcelona (Espanya station) and Manresa link to the cog railway *(cremallera funicular)* and the cable car up to the monastery of Montserrat. You can purchase a single ticket for both the train and the cog railway or for the train and the cable car. The tickets are not interchangeable. There are also tickets that include an additional cog railway ride from the monastery to the top of the mountain.

You can visit Montserrat with a guided one-day bus tour from Barcelona. This option may be the easiest, but you will have limited freedom to explore the monastery and the mountainside.

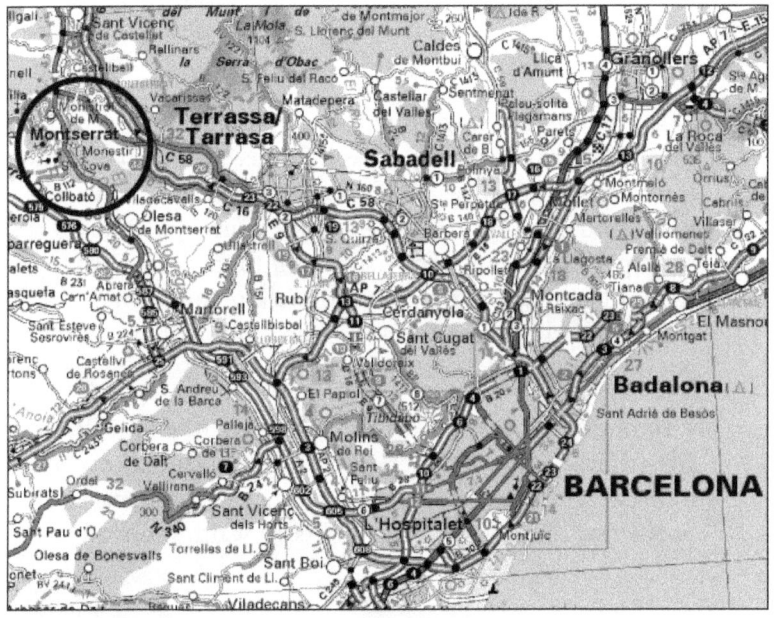

Map of the area

We highly recommend an overnight visit to Montserrat. In the evening, Montserrat empties of visitors and you will have more time to absorb the atmosphere of this fascinating sacred site. Hotel and restaurant accommodations are quite good. If you arise early in the morning you can enjoy the views as the sun rises over the mountains as well as make an early morning visit to Our Lady's chapel.

Cable car ascending Montserrat

The traditional way of getting to Montserrat is on foot. After all, it is a pilgrimage shrine. Well-marked trails from Monistrol and Collbató take less than two hours and offer exciting views of the countryside. Go to http://www.montserratvisita.com/ for details about the trail system. Please note: the walk requires a very stiff uphill climb and is not for those who are not in good physical condition.

In our opinion, the least advantageous way to visit Montserrat is by car. There is limited parking at the monastery and cars are only admitted when a space opens up. This can result in hours of waiting on the narrow, twisting road—and occasionally exciting maneuvers to permit large tour busses to get by. (http://www.sacred-destinations.com/spain/montserrat-shrine)

Notes

Dolmen de la Cova d'en Daina

Dolmen de la Cova d'en Daina, Romanyà de la Sélva, Baix Empordà

The dolmen Cova d'en Daina is close to the highway but distant enough from town that it is not over-run with tourists. We walk a short distance to a clearing in a forest dotted with lichen-covered boulders. There stands the dolmen surrounded by a low wall of ancient upright stones. We walk three times around, then spend time being present to the stones, noting the energy lines that cross at the entrance to the chamber. After "introducing" myself to the dolmen, I sit quietly on the capstone and meditate. Suddenly I enter an altered reality. Trees and stones waiver from view as I drift into another time, another place. Back I go—or maybe forward—through the centuries. Abruptly, voices break my concentration: a British couple is asking Gary how to use the dowsing rods... (Elyn)

> "We need to start thinking of ancient monuments as memory banks in the landscape: after all, as consciousness researcher, John Steele, has pointed out, the very word 'monument' derives from a Latin term meaning 'to remind.'" Paul Devereux. *Earth Memory: Sacred Sites—Doorways into Earth's Mysteries*. St. Paul: Llewellyn Publications, 1992, p. 16.

East side of the dolmen

The dolmen de la Cova d'en Daina (COH-vuh don DIE-na) (The Cave of Daina) is a four- or five-thousand-year-old passage "tomb" constructed of twenty-five large granite slabs surrounded by a circular stone wall of the same material. This wall once encircled a mound of earth that covered the gallery and chamber, making the whole structure a tumulus, similar to those found in Brittany and Ireland, among other places. Remains of the earthen mound are still visible, although the mound no longer covers the central structure. Ninteenth-century excavations of Cova d'en Daina revealed human bones and teeth, along with fragments of knives, ceramics, and more than 300 large stone necklaces.

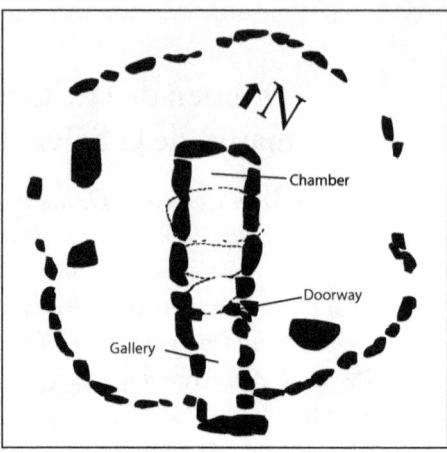

Plan of Cova d'en Daina

It is not accurate to call these sites "tombs," although some of them, including Cova d'en Daina, were used as graves. They were also much more, including (at times) ceremonial centers and powerful places for the people who built them. Earth-energy researchers have suggested that these sites may have been used for increasing the fertility of crops or for healing purposes. It's easy to discover material evidence—much harder to rediscover exactly how ancient people

> "The ancient people who discovered the power places and erected structures at them quite probably related with the sites through both feeling and knowing. If contemporary people wish to access the energy fields of the sacred sites they should likewise use both knowing and feeling." Martin Grey. *Sacred and Magical Places*. On his website http://www.sacredsites.com.

View down the gallery from inside the central chamber

utilized the energies of sacred sites.

The dolmen is twenty-five feet in length and approximately six feet wide. The outer circle is thirty-six feet in diameter. The chamber is rectangular; there is a low doorway between the gallery and the chamber. Originally, capstones covered the entire structure, but only three are still in place. The remains of the others may be nearby. We noticed a stone lying in front of the main entrance that might have originally been situated above.

When we dowsed the site we found an energy line that enters through the outer doorway of the dolmen and traverses the entire length. Another energy line crosses the first at the doorway between the gallery and the chamber. The gallery and chamber face south-southeast, probably lining up

Our friend Anne, meditating on the capstone

with the rising sun at winter or summer solstices. This southeast orientation is quite common for dolmens. The master builders must have chosen

> Remember that in approaching any sacred site it is best to introduce yourself. Try using BLESSING and ECOLOGY as suggested in "Experiencing a Powerful Place" on pp. 9-11. Simple techniques like these will pay dividends in increased awareness and enjoyment.

the site to connect with both the rising sun and the underground energies.

Meditating while sitting on the capstone of the dolmen produced a powerful effect. Try it and see what you experience.

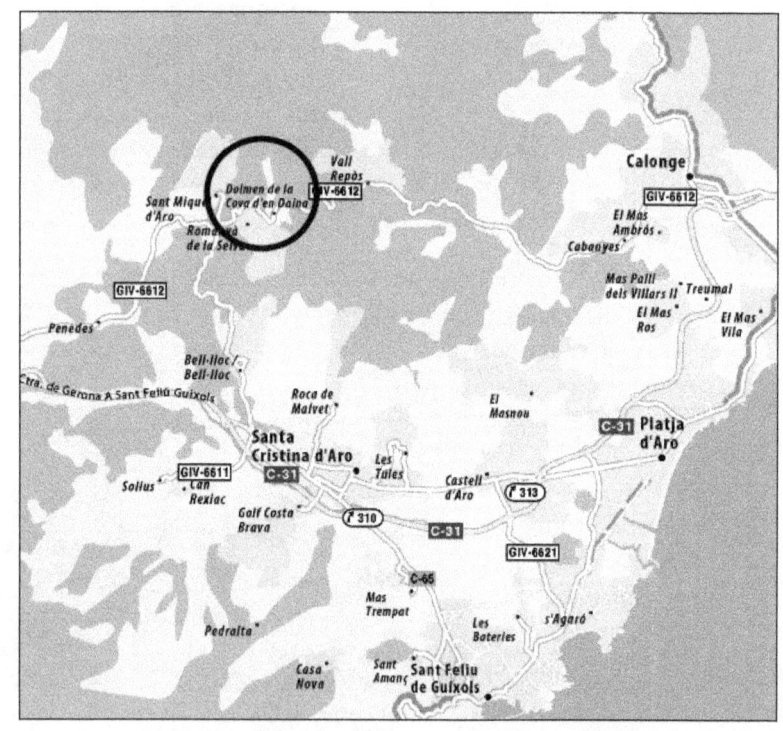

Area map

Signpost

Two middle-aged couples came to visit the dolmen while we were there. One woman said, "I grew up near here. We all believed that if you go inside the dolmen you'll have good luck." So, with a smile, she crawled inside and so did her woman friend. She said that she had been visiting the dolmen since she was a child. This association of the dolmen with good luck is an interesting example of how folklore retains the memory of the power of a place long after the details have been forgotten.

Getting to Cova d'en Daina

Drive fifteen and one-half miles south of Girona on C-65 and turn north on GIV-6612 toward Romanyà de la Selva. Cova d'en Daina is on the left after passing through the town and about three and one-half miles from the turn-off. A signpost clearly marks the site.

Notes

The Old Quarter

Girona (Gerona), Gironès

Its siren call lures me again and again. Each time I leave, I feel as if I've missed something—as if there's another secret lurking behind a closed doorway or a bend in the ancient city walls, hiding in a ruined turret or in the faint traces of a tower now inexplicably removed from the Frenchwoman's Garden. I wander through the old city, exploring tiny, twisted alleys in what once was the Jewish quarter, the Call, fabled center of medieval esotericism, birthplace in 1194 of Moses ben Nahman, a.k.a. Nahmanides or Bonastruc ça Porta, the famous Kabbalist. The name resounds through the centuries, five hundred years after the Jews were evicted from their homes.

When I tire of such explorations, I head down to the River Onyar, its banks lined with colorful buildings. I sit at a shady sidewalk café and watch pedestrians cross one of the many bridges that unite the Barri Vell (Old Quarter) with the new city. Girona is a bit like Venice without the crowds, without the gondolas, without the smell—and with much more mystery. (Elyn)

An important and strategic city in Roman times, Girona (zjhee-ROW-nuh) began as a fortress town called Gerunda, which guarded the confluence of four rivers: Ter, Güell, Galligants, and Onyar. The Carrer de Força, which passes through the Old Quarter, was a major Roman communication route called Via Augusta. In the third century CE Girona was invaded by Franks and Germans and later by Visigoths. Muslims held power briefly until Charlemagne reconquered the city in 785 and made it one of the fourteen counties in his Catalan empire. There was a flourishing Jewish community in Girona in the eleventh to thirteenth centuries. Rabbi Moses ben Nahman Gerondi (better known as Nahmanides) established a Kabbalah school that was one of the most important in Europe. Jews were expelled from Catalunya in 1492. The Jewish quarter, the Call (CAHee), was forgotten but not destroyed; it is among the largest and best-preserved Jewish districts in Europe.

Girona endured twenty-five sieges and was captured seven times in its long history. In 1809 it fell to Napoleon's armies and was a part of France until 1813. The defensive city walls were demolished at the end of the nineteenth century to make room for expansion, but they have been reconstructed and are a favorite tourist route around the old city. Modern-day Girona is

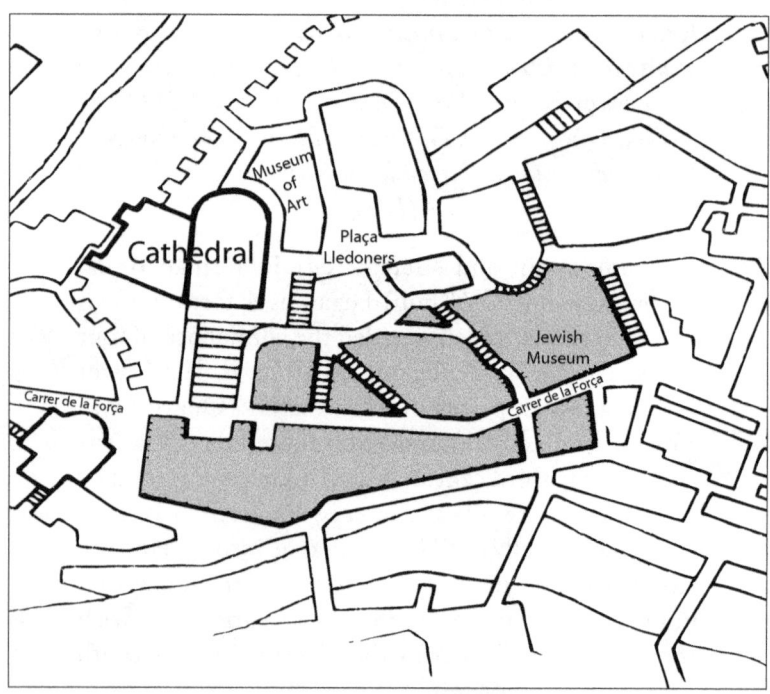

The Old Quarter of Girona
The Call is highlighted

a cosmopolitan city reflecting the many cultures that have flourished there over the centuries.

The Call and Old Girona

The Barri Vell (bah-ree VAY-uh) or Old Quarter of Girona is most picturesque, filled with small boutiques, restaurants, and bars. The narrow streets and stairways perfectly evoke a medieval town and are endlessly fascinating. The Call lies at the very heart of the district and includes the Bonastruc ça Porta Centre, with its Jewish History Museum and Nahmanides Institute.

A street in the Call

The museum is a must-see, with excellent displays of medieval Jewish life. It occupies the building that until 1492 housed the synagogue and other Jewish communal areas. The Barri Vell is a very powerful place. As you wander through narrow streets and

Courtyard of the Jewish Museum

covered alleyways, ignore the modern shop windows and tourists, and see if you can return to the Middle Ages for a few moments. You may even hear the faint whispers of learned arguments or feel the lingering energy of Kabbalistic practices. (The cover of this book is a photo taken in the Call.)

Another street in the Call

The Cathedral

Between the Call and the city walls lies the impressive (widest Gothic nave in the world) cathedral of Girona. We find the areas around the cathedral more interesting than the building itself, but there are two items inside that should not be missed. One is the "Throne of Charlemagne," a marble throne dating from the eleventh century—well after Charlemagne's death in 814—and the other is the Tapestry of the Creation. This rare textile measures fifteen feet by twelve feet and is in amazingly good condition. The intricate design is wool, embroidered on a rough linen base. It depicts the Pantocrator (Christ the Ruler) in the center and includes the stages of creation, the four winds, the passing seasons, the months of the year, and the rivers and mountains of paradise. We can't show it to you in color, so

View from the city walls

> "Girona holds on to its atmosphere and makes sure the past is there always, solid, unconquered by decay. It was said the stones had a magnetism that drew certain people back time and time again. I believe it. Carcassonne has the same legend and I've heard it's to do with the ley lines. At certain points across the earth the energy builds up and creates a pull, a pulse, and in these places unusual and mystical things can happen." Patrice Chaplin. *City of Secrets*. Wheaton, IL: Quest Books, 2008, p. 6.

you will have to go to Girona and see it for yourself. It is stunning.

The City Walls

One of the best ways to see Girona is by walking the extensive city walls that begin near the cathedral and encircle the Old Quarter, ending with an overlook to the River Onyar. Parts of the walls were reconstructed in the twentieth century, providing wonderful views into the city. There are opportunities along the walk to descend to the gardens below. We will highlight two of these gardens.

The Frenchwoman's Garden

We were introduced to the Frenchwoman's Garden by reading Patrice Chaplin's *City of Secrets* (see grey box above). In this stream-of-consciousness autobiographical work Chaplin describes a mysterious quasi-Masonic cult that she believes flourished in Girona in the nineteenth and twentieth centuries. The Frenchwoman's house figures prominently in Chaplin's book and is connected with the French priest Bérenger

The Frenchwoman's Garden

Saunière, who in the final years of the nineteenth century spent a fortune restoring the church in his little parish in Rennes-le-Château in the Languedoc region of France. He also built a mansion beside the church and a tower that he called the "Tour Magdala" to house his library. No one knows where Saunière got his wealth; the Rennes-le-Château mystery has been the subject of several books and television documentaries.

> "Modern science tells us that what we commonly call 'reality' is a compilation of pictures based on a narrow sense-band view of surface features. The world we perceive is a small slice of a vast, mostly invisible energy-event." Michael S. Schneider. *A Beginner's Guide to Constructing the Universe - The Mathematical Archetypes of Nature, Art, and Science.* HarperPerennial Edition, 1995., p. xxiii.

In *City of Secrets* Chaplin produces evidence that Abbé Saunière was a regular visitor to the house of the Frenchwoman in Girona and that he carried on a correspondence with Maria Tourdes, the Frenchwoman who lived in this house. Furthermore, there was a tower in the city wall behind her house that appears to be an exact duplicate of Abbé Saunière's Tour Magdala at Rennes-le-Château. Chaplin has documents supposedly in Saunière's hand of a drawing of the towers and suggests that the Abbé modeled his tower on the one in Girona. You will have to read Chaplin's book to see what she makes of all this.

Fountain in the Frenchwoman's Garden

Today the house and the tower are

Gargoyle on the cathedral—visible from the Frenchwoman's Garden

both gone and the site is identified on city maps as The Frenchwoman's Garden (Jardins de la Francesa). It is a small garden on two levels, tucked into the city wall overlooking the cathedral. There is some evidence on the site as to where the house and tower were; you can compare the old photographs in Chaplin's book to see more. We observed that a major energy line that passes down the central aisle of the cathedral crosses the garden. Our sense was that this place is a powerful place but not a happy one. Perhaps our perceptions were colored by having read Chaplin's book. See what you experience there.

The German Garden

The German Garden is much larger than the Frenchwoman's Garden and filled with extensive plantings. It is a beautiful oasis in the center of the city and worth a visit when you walk the walls.

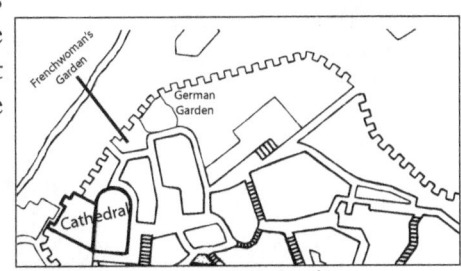

The Frenchwoman's Garden and the German Garden

Sant Pere de Galligants and Archeology Museum

Split-tailed mermaid on a capital in the cloister of the Archeology Museum

The ancient Benedictine monastery of Sant Pere de Galligants is the home of Girona's Archeology Museum. The twelfth-century church is an exquisite Romanesque building with beautiful sculpture throughout. The capitals in the cloister are worthy of note. We found the cloister to be a powerful place. The siren-mermaid capital, with two eyes in its pelvis, is intriguing. (You'll find similar split-tailed mermaids in other Romanesque churches—they're worth looking for and contemplating.....) The exhibits in the museum are of interest to those who enjoy learning about the early history of people in Iberia.

> "According to church doctrine, the siren-mermaid symbolizes the sin of lust. I wondered if the split-tailed female was a variant of the Sheela-na-Gig a figurative carving of a naked woman (often skeletal in appearance) squatting with knees apart, one or both hands spreading wide her exaggerated vulva." Elyn Aviva. *Walking Through Cancer: A Pilgrimage of Gratitude on the Way of St. James.* Santa Fe: Pilgrims Process, Inc., 2009, pp. 139-140. (See *Powerful Places in Scotland*, p. 34, for more on Sheela-na-gig.)

Area map

Other Things to Do and See

Girona is a lively city with many opportunities to please travelers. La Rambla, which parallels the river, is the city's social main street, with all the shops, restaurants, street performers, etc. that you would expect in a major tourist destination. The historic Arab Baths (not Arab and no longer baths) are worth a visit. Across the river from the Old Quarter you will find the Plaça de la Independència and Mercadal District, which is the center for upscale shopping. Other interesting museums include the Museum of the History of the City, The Cinema Museum, the Art Museum, and the historic Pharmacy of Santa Caterina. The nightlife in both the Old Quarter and the Plaça de la Independència is memorable, as is the gastronomy.

(http://www.girona-tourist-guide.com/ http://www.girona.cat/call/eng/)

Getting There

Girona is sixty-three miles northeast of Barcelona. It can be easily reached by train, or you can fly into the Girona-Costa Brava airport south of the city. We don't recommend driving in the Old Quarter of Girona, but there is ample parking in the newer parts of the city. The Old Quarter and the new district across the river are quite walkable.

Notes

Horsecart ride in the Beech Forest (La Fageda d'en Jordà)

La Garrotxa, Garrotxa

La Garrotxa: a region filled with intriguing villages, hermitages, hiking trails, springs, and over forty tree-covered hills. A surprising reality is disguised behind the bucolic appearances—they're not hills, they're volcanoes! Not lava-spewing volcanoes, admittedly, but quiet, slumbering ones. A network of trails leads to several of them, and there is at least one you can walk into. It was a steep pull, but we made it to the top of Santa Margarida in about 25 minutes. A narrow trail leads down to the tiny stone hermitage nestling in the bottom of the crater. The energy was sweet, protective—and energizing. I wondered: why build a hermitage inside a crater? That wasn't the only mystery we would discover.

*The next day we strolled through La Fageda d'en Jordà, a magical beech forest in the midst of a volcanic field. The trees grow on large (and small) volcanic hillocks, their roots clinging to lumps of moss-covered scoria. Autumn-hued leaves swayed in the breeze like Kabuki dancers. Later, at lunch in the "Jack and the Beanstalk" restaurant, we noticed ceramic figures—*follet *magics—for sale. The waitress explained that* follet *is Catalan for* duende *(elf) and that "people say" there are* duendes *and* fadas *(fairies) in the forest. I was not surprised. The forest is alive; magic is afoot. (Elyn)*

La Garrotxa (la gah-RAHT-cha), a 280-square-mile county *(comtat)* northwest of Girona, is divided in two parts by the river Fluvia. The upper zone, called Alta Garrotxa (Upper Garrotxa), is mountainous, while the lower zone, sometimes called Olot after the capital city, contains the Natural Park of the Volcanic Zone (Parc Natural de la Zona Volcànica de la

Garrotxa). The Alta Garrotxa is an important area in the eastern pre-Pyrenees because of its diversity and exceptional surroundings. It is extremely mountainous and has sheltered many types of vegetation and fauna, allowing them to continue to flourish in relative isolation. It has been declared a Space of Natural Interest and has been designated as a Zone of Special Protection for Birds by Natura 2000 (http://www.natura.org).

La Garrotxa

The lower zone of La Garrotxa contains the 45-square-mile Volcanic Park, which includes the towns of Olot and Santa Pau and the beech forest, as well as forty well-preserved volcanic cones and extensive lava flows. The largest lava field covers over ten square miles. However, you won't find smoking craters and black fields of congealed lava here. The most recent eruption was that of the Volcà de Croscat, which took place 11,500 years ago, making it the youngest Iberian volcano. Numerous park trails enable you to appreciate the un-

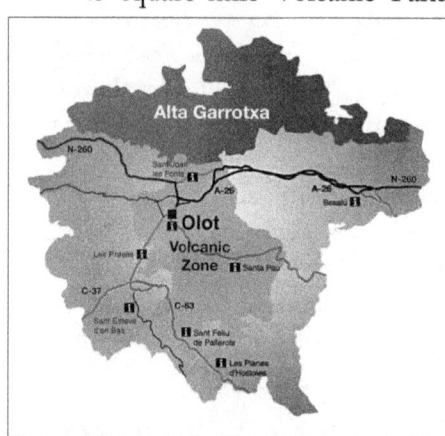

Alta Garrotxa and the Volcanic Zone

usual tree-covered landscape. In this section, we will concentrate on the lower zone.

The Beech Forest

The Beech Forest (La Fageda d'en Jordà) (la fuh-ZJEH-duh don ZJOR-dah) is an extensive stand of beech trees growing on the ancient Croscat lava flow. Beech forests don't normally grow at this low altitude, but they do very well in this volcanic soil. We were privileged to be there at the height of autumn, when the ground and trees were bathed in glowing, golden light. It was a magical experience. The well-known Catalan poet, Joan Maragall (1860-1911), catches the spirit of this place in his poem "La Fageda d'en Jordà" (see grey box on the following page). There is a monument to Maragall in the forest and one of the shorter walking paths is named after him.

The trees are beautiful, but the ground on which they grow is also stunning. Scattered amongst the beeches are chunks of lava rock and moss-covered volcanic hillocks. The boulders were thrown up in explosions of steam that collected in the cooling Coscat lava field. The roughness of the tumbled ter-

A hillock in the Beech Forest

rain has been muted over the centuries by a gentle covering of trees, ivy, and moss. This definitely felt like a place where the fairies and "the little people" lived—and maybe they still do.

We saw elf and witch figures for sale, and restaurants with names like "El Follet" (The Elf). At first we wondered if this was due to ancient Celtic influence. Then Elyn realized that you don't have to have Celtic influence to have elves and fairies—stories about them are found all over the world! In other words, the elves and fairies came first, then people noticed them and incorporated them into their folklore. We tried to find out about local myths and legends at the tourist office, but the woman in charge vehemently denied that there were any legends about elves and fairies; the figures, she said, were mere tourist souvenirs. (Later we found a book in Catalan about elves, fairies, and

La Fageda d'en Jordà by Joan Maragall

Do you know where the Beechwood Forest of Jordà is?
If you go to the environs of Olot, above the plain,
you'll encounter a place, green and intense,
like nowhere else you have encountered in the world:
a green like inland water, deep and clear;
the green of the Beechwood Forest of Jordà.
The traveller who enters this place,
begins to walk slowly;
Counting his steps in the great stillness:
He stops, and feels nothing, and is lost.
He is gripped by a sweet forgetfulness of everything
in the silence of that deep place,
and doesn't think of leaving, or thinks in vain:
he is taken by the Beechwood Forest of Jordà,
prisoner of the silence and the green.
Oh company! Oh liberating jail!

other creatures in the region, so the folklore does exist....)

Whatever the truth of the matter (or the origin of the legends) it is clear that Maragall became enchanted while walking through the forest. Perhaps this was the work of "the little people." Take a walk in La Fageda d'en Jordà and see what you encounter.

Santa Margarida

A hermitage in the center of a volcanic crater? Why hide it there? To make the journey more arduous and hence more worthwhile? To take advantage of the peculiar telluric energies within the crater? Perhaps the point was seclusion from the outside world. To reach the hermitage of Santa Margarida you must climb up the Santa Margarida Volcano (Volcà de Santa Margarida), with a 460-foot rise in elevation. The trail is

Santa Margarida Volcano and hermitage

wide and well maintained, but it is steep. At the top you descend about 150 feet into the crater to the hermitage located in a meadow at the bottom. The walk is well worth the effort, even though the hermitage is usually closed.

Saint Margaret is noticed by Olybrius

The hermitage is dedicated to St. Margaret (Santa Margarida, in Catalan) of Antioch, who may have been martyred in the early fourth century. Her legend, which parallels that of several other early virgin martyrs, relates that she was a Christian who had dedicated her virginity to God. Unfortunately, the shepherdess attracted the attention of Olybrius, a Roman prefect, who desired her as his concubine. When she refused his advances and refused to recant her Christian beliefs, she was tortured

> "Since the dawn of human time people have described certain places as being holy or magical, as having a concentrated power or presence of spirit. Ancient legends, historical records and contemporary reports tell of extraordinary, even miraculous happenings at these places - the sick are healed, deities appear, artists receive inspiration, prophets see visions and sages attain spiritual enlightenment. It is a curious fact, however, that these sacred sites, so significant to human culture, are so little known beyond their own religious traditions. Of enormous importance, they have received only limited attention from social anthropologists, cultural geographers and religious historians. Why this remarkable omission of awareness and understanding?" Martin Gray. "Sacred Earth Journeys Newsletter," March/April 2004.

and beheaded. St. Margaret is widely venerated as a patron of pregnant women.

Santa Pau

Santa Pau is a charming thirteenth-century village in the heart of the Garrotxa volcanic region. We found it a convenient base for our explorations. The medieval walled town, built on a hill with an abandoned castle in the center, has excellent dining and lodging facilities. It has been declared a historical and artistic monument.

Santa Pau at night

Wandering the narrow streets of Santa Pau is a pleasant experience. There is a well-marked walk along the city walls, quite evocative at night, that passes by medieval city gates, stone houses, and mysterious alleys. There are also descriptive plaques located at scenic overlooks. In the newer (eighteenth-century) section of the town, across the bridge, is a row of houses with intriguingly carved lintels. Various symbols seem to indicate the professions of the buildings' proprietors; some look like Masonic symbols.

See http://www.turismegarrotxa.com/_en.html and http://www.i-santapau.com.

Other Things to Do and See

La Garrotxa is a popular Catalan vacation destination. As such, it features numerous tourist activities. There are horse cart rides through La Fageda d'en Jordà, hot air balloon rides over the entire area, horseback trips, and a miniature train that departs from one of the campgrounds (Camping Lava). Olot has a number of interesting museums, including the Museum of the Volcanoes.

The area offers a variety of outdoor adventures. The 30-mile-long Carrilet cycling path (which follows an old railway line) goes from Girona to Olot. The region is crisscrossed with 28 Itinerànnia hiking trails, a network of well-marked paths that recreates the historical tracks and trails that once linked all the settlements in the region. The tourist office at Can Serra, the main entrance to the Beech Forest, provides free walking brochures. Complete routes are available in *Itinerànnia Garrotxa,* a guidebook and topographical map published by Editorial Alpina. For a very different experience, visit La Fageda, a local farm and dairy at the edge of the Beech Forest. It produces commercial grades of yogurt products (La Fageda) and is staffed by developmentally disabled people. There are regular guided tours.

Because La Garrotxa is such a popular vacation spot, plan your visit to avoid the summer high season and weekends in early fall.

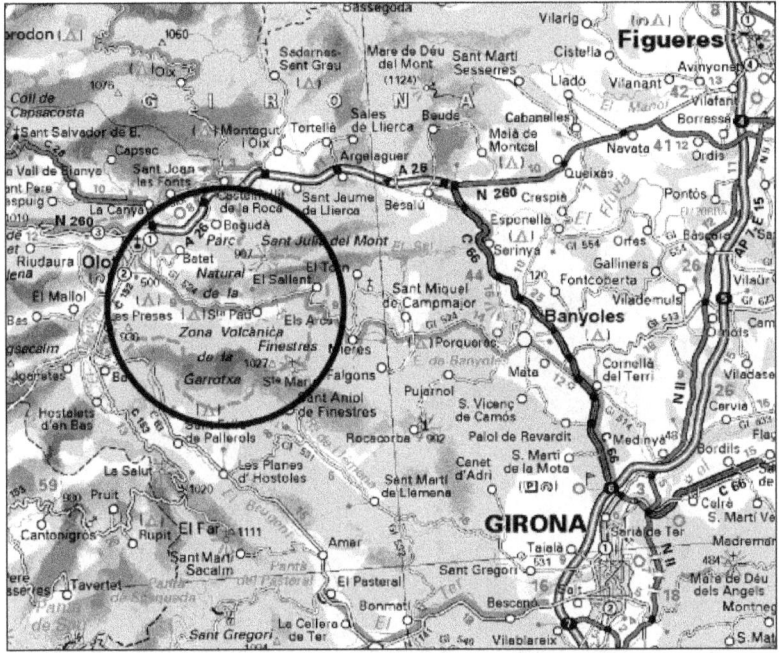

Area map

Getting There

There is excellent bus service to the Olot urban area from Barcelona, Girona, Figueres, Ripoll, and Vic, run by the TEISA bus company (http://www.teisa-bus.com). There are no railway connections to the region, but you can take trains to one of the cities mentioned above and use the bus service from there. To really see La Garrotxa you need a car, so taking the train to one of the major cities or flying into Girona-Costa Brava Airport and renting a car would be a good option. You can also get around by bike. The local busses usually permit bikes on board, but you should check beforehand to make sure.

Calvary—Descent from the Cross

Sant Joan de les Abadesses, Ripollès

We reach Sant Joan de les Abadesses and park next to the Romanesque church that bears the same name. We stroll around the outside of the apse, enjoying the amusing Romanesque capitals of beard-pullers (a sign of lust?) and paired elephants that, along with other sculpted oddities, adorn the walls. Inside, the stark thirteenth-century wooden Calvary depicting the descent of Christ from the cross looks like a modern Giacometti sculpture. The Gothic cloister delights me with its delicate twinned columns—the most elegant I have ever seen. Unexpectedly, tears fill my eyes.

The energy of the church is definitely feminine, which is not surprising since Wilfred the Hairy founded the monastery in 885 for his baby daughter Emma, the first abbess. I wonder how she felt about having her religious vocation chosen for her at such a tender age. Perhaps, given the times, it wasn't such a bad choice. (Elyn)

The founding of Sant Joan de les Abadesses (St. John of the Abbesses) was part of Wilfred the Hairy's plan for the reconquest and repopulation of Spain following the defeat of the Moors in 718. The early group of monastic buildings must have looked more like a fort than a religious institution. It was referred to as the "Castle of St. Joan" in early documents. The repopulation of Catalunya was successful and this was, in part, due to efforts of the nuns of St. Joan. Over the years, they established a number of churches in surrounding areas, thus establishing new population centers.

The later history of St. Joan is rife with political intrigue. In 1017 the monastery was dissolved after a series of accusations by Bernat Tallaferro of misconduct by the nuns; it soon reopened as a community for men with Tallaferro's stepbrother, Ingilberga, as bishop. The strife continued until the beginning of the twelfth century, when Augustinian rule was established.

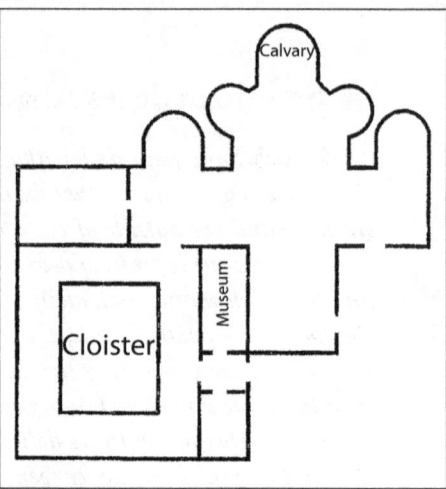

Floor plan of the church

The present buildings were constructed in the twelfth and thirteenth centuries. Strangely, the addition of the name "Abadesses" came at the same time. Earlier documents had not referred to it by that title.

The monastery established the town of Sant Joan de les Abadesses in the thirteenth century. The streets are regular and parallel with each other, a sure sign of urban planning. The following centuries were marked by devastation from the Black Plague in 1348, an earthquake in 1428, unsuccessful siege by the French in 1484, demolition of the cloister in 1620, capture by Napoleon's troops in 1809, siege of the Seven Year War in 1837, and destruction of the church in 1936 during the

The cloister in Sant Joan de les Abadesses

Choir stall arm rests in museum—wild boar playing bagpipes

Civil War. The present buildings are a skillful reconstruction that was completed in the 1970s. During the late nineteenth and early twentieth century the poet Joan Maragall (see pp. 62, 76) made his home near the monastery.

We found the fifteenth-century cloister to be a very powerful place. The delicacy of the twin columns supporting gothic arches and their elegant style makes it one of the more striking cloisters we have visited. We didn't want to leave.

The capitals, both inside and outside the church, are intriguing. Fantastic animal figures vie with scenes from the Bible and floral designs. Of particular interest are two capitals showing men pulling their beards. In both cases the figures are bi-corporal (having two bodies). Beard-pulling figures are said to represent the sin of lust, but maybe that's just "pulling your beard!"

Inside, the church is austere, delicate in feeling, and sweet. Of note is a thirteenth-century sculptural group of the Descent from

Lions holding onto a tree

the Cross. The seven almost-lifesize figures are striking in their realism and emotion. In 1426 a Eucharist wafer was discovered in perfect condition in a cavity in the forehead of the Christ figure. This has given it the name "Sacred Mystery." The sacred host disappeared in 1936.

Other Things to Do and See

The museum inside the church is tiny but well worth visiting. There are interesting examples of early textiles in the collection. Don't miss the Renaissance choir stall arm rests, which include a wild boar playing the bagpipes (see p. 71), a monkey playing the flute and drum, and a fox with a hen.

Traveling east from Sant Joan de les Abadesses you can visit Olot and La Garrotxa (see pp. 58-67). Traveling west you can visit a number of Romanesque churches. The Monastery of Santa Maria in Ripoll has one of the best-preserved Romanesque portals in Spain. In the Toses region you can visit Sant Martí de Fornells, Sant Víctor de Dòrria with its Romanesque paintings, Sant Cristòfol de Nevà, Sant Cristòfol de Toses also with Romanesque paintings, Sant Marel de Planès, and Sant Vicenç de Planoles, all Romanesque churches. In Puigcerdà is the former convent of Sant Domènec. Exquisite wall paintings in a number of churches in the region have been removed to the National Museum of Catalan Art (MNAC) in Barcelona. Some of these feature the Virgin holding a flaming chalice.

For those interested in hiking, the former railroad lines in the area have been made into a series of hiking trails. See http://www.gironagreenways.org/

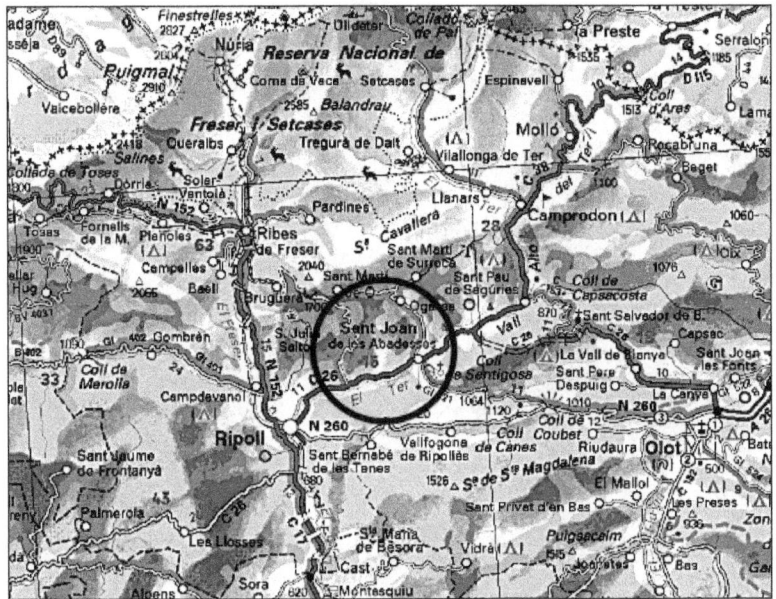

Area map

Getting There

There is no train service in this area, but bus service is available from Ripoll, Barcelona, and Olot. However, you will need a car to explore the surrounding areas so renting a car in Barcelona or Girona might be the best plan.

Notes

Stained glass window of the Virgin of Núria

Vall de Núria, Ripollès

We rode on the cremallera *("zipper" train) up into the high Pyrenees—a route featuring breathtaking views at every vertiginous twist and turn on a track too steep to ascend or descend any other way. After a short ride that felt long, we reached the bowl-shaped valley of the Sanctuary of Núria. Winter sports facilities, a cable car leading up to a mountaintop, and a massive sanctuary, complete with hostel for the many tourists and pilgrims who come on foot or by train, greeted us.*

Despite the unaesthetic buildings, the chapel of la Virgen de Núria is an oasis of peace and serenity. Center of all attention, seated on a throne, she looks out from behind a large glass window high above the nave. We climbed the stairs that lead to her elevated nook and circumambulated her Plexiglas cage. A blue ribbon ending with a medal dangles from her throne, granting surrogate access to her miracle-working power. While I watched, a mother showed her little girl how to kiss the medal while the pale-faced Virgin stared straight ahead. I contemplated the politics of appearance: recent restoration has transformed this once-dark Virgin into white. (Elyn)

Isolated and nearly inaccessible except by cog railway, the valley of the river Núria (Vall de Núria) is a high alpine meadow at the end of a challenging 3,300-foot ascent through the narrow 7¾-mile-long river gorge. It has been a very popular winter sports area in Catalunya for well over a half century, ever since the cog railway was finished in 1931. To make the 40-minute trip through this gorge on the slow-moving train is a thrilling experience in itself, but that is only the beginning. The valley is stunning.

When we arrived at the Vall de Núria our first impression was that it is like a major US ski resort—think Aspen or Vail in the Rocky Mountains. There are hotels, campgrounds, restaurants, a children's playground, and shops. The massive sanctuary complex, begun at the end of the nineteenth century and finished in 1956, was hardly appealing. Was that all there was? Then we entered the sanctuary and encountered the loving presence of the Virgen de Núria.

The zipper train

The Sanctuary of the Virgin of Núria

According to legend, Sant Gil (Saint Giles, Bishop of Nîmes) established a hermitage in the Vall de Núria between 700-703 CE. He sculpted an image of the Virgin and used a bell to call the local shepherds to hear him preach. He also fed them from a copper cooking pot. When he fled the valley, he hid the statue of the Virgin, the cross, the bell, and the copper pot. In 1072, a Syrian named Amadeo came from Dalmatia after an angel told him in a dream to go to Núria, build a chapel for the Virgin, and find the hidden

> **Praise to the Virgin of Núria**
> **by Joan Maragall**
> Stanza IV
> In winter, when it's snowing and raining,
> and the city tosses and turns
> sparkling with insomnia and rage,
> our dazzled eyes
> will see, there in the darkness,
> the motionless Virgin of Núria
> ensconced in solitude.

The sanctuary complex today

treasures. The angel said a white stone marked the hiding place. Amadeo built a small chapel for the Virgin but left before finding the treasures. Seven years later a shepherd saw a red bull striking a stone wall with its hoof. When the wall was broken open there was a resplendent light coming from the statue of the Virgin within; beside her were the cross, the bell, and the copper pot—which became the symbols of Núria.

Modern scholarship dates the Virgin of Núria from the end of the twelfth century or early thirteenth century—not the eighth. No one knows if the current statue is a copy of an earlier one or not, but the current Virgin has been credited with numerous fertility miracles over the centuries. Many couples have come to the shrine, prayed before the cross, placed their heads in the pot, rung the bell—and been granted offspring. One folklorist points out that the original white stone in the valley was probably a menhir with fertility associations. The Christian shrine has substituted the pot for the stone, and the tradition continues.

The small chapel of the Virgin, high above the nave, is

The Virgin of Núria

quite powerful. We dowsed a crossing of fire and water lines in front of the Virgin that generated "energetic steam." The presence of these lines is intriguing since this is not the original location of the Virgin; that was destroyed and the Virgin moved to her current setting in 1911. The present church is at right angles and on a different site from the original church.

Interior of the church with the Virgin above

The Virgin of Núria holds a special place in the hearts of Catalans. In 1932 the Republican Generalitat de Catalunya met in the Vall de Núria to draft the Statute of 1932, which proclaimed Catalunya as an autonomous country. This "Statute of Núria" was never recognized in Madrid, however, and the Virgin of Núria became a symbol of insubordination to General Franco.

> The face of the Virgin after restoration in 2000 is white, but earlier photos and drawings show it as black—or as white. Although it is listed as a Black Virgin in Ean Begg's gazetteer, perhaps he jumped to conclusions and, in this case, the darkness really *was* the result of centuries of smoke. After all, before restoration even her clothes looked black. (According to one source, restoration in 1799 of the famous Swiss Black Virgin of Einsiedeln revealed a white face beneath the soot, but the congregation demanded that she be restored to black.....)

> "Throughout Spain, some images [of Black Virgins] were created black, some were blackened later, some lost their polychrome or are in natural wood (often called brown Virgins), many are now whitened, some are white but have typically 'black' stories and shapes." Ean Begg. *The Cult of the Black Virgin*. Revised and expanded edition. London: Penguin Books, 1985, p. 281.

During the 1936-1939 Civil War the statue was secretly moved into France and later Switzerland to protect it from Franco's militia. It was returned in 1941 but was kidnapped in 1967, this time by Catalan patriots who were protesting the appointment of non-Catalan bishops. The Virgin was returned in 1972 on the day that a Catalan bishop was appointed to the Barcelona seat. The Virgin of Núria is a powerful symbol both of miraculous intervention and of Catalan politics.

The Hermitage of Sant Gil

The oldest extant building in the Vall de Núria is the Hermitage of Saint Giles (La Casa de Sant Gil), located across the river from the main buildings. Dating from 1615, this small chapel has an altar, a niche for prayers, and a reliquary. It is built on the site where the hidden treasures were supposedly found. The structure was restored in 2003. We found this to be a powerful place.

Other Things to Do and See

The high alpine meadows of the Vall de Núria are home to an extensive array

The Hermitage of Sant Gil

of flora and fauna that live 6,500 feet above sea level. The valley has been developed to adhere to international ISO 14004 standards for environmental sustainability to ensure that succeeding generations who visit the area, whether for sports or on spiritual pilgrimage, will find it much as it is today. An extensive system of hiking trails offer opportunities to enjoy the valley in spring, summer, and fall. For those who are interested in winter sports, a ski resort provides lifts and slopes of all levels of difficulty. You can go skating and snowboarding, and there are hotel and restaurant facilities.

The original site of the treasures

A stop en route at Queralbs is worthwhile. A typical Pyreneen village, it features a tenth-century church dedicated to Sant Jaume—also known as St. James or Santiago. Stone houses and cobblestone streets give it a picturesque appearance.

Nearby Ripoll is an interesting town with a very important Romanesque church façade. We home-based there for our trip to Vall de Núria.

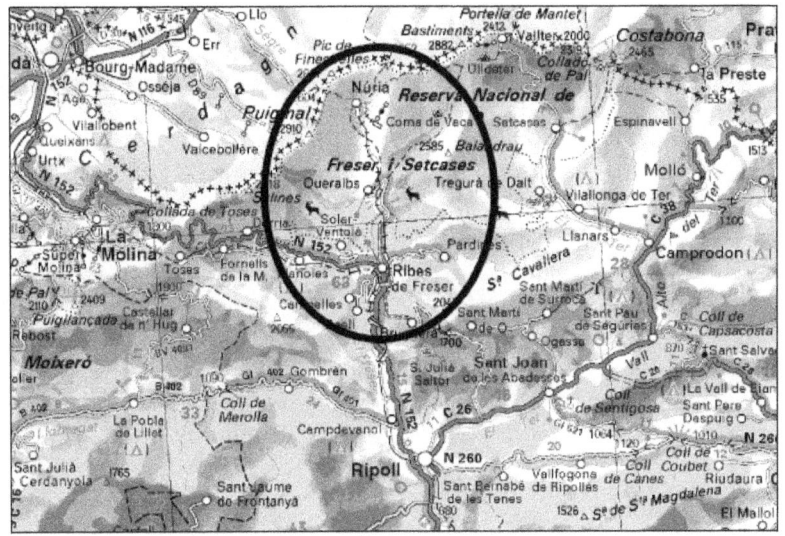

Area map

Getting There

There are only two ways to get to the Vall de Núria—on foot or by cog railway. For those who want to walk we recommend buying a good hiking map and guidebook. The cog railway *(cremallera)* begins at the Ribes-Enllaç station, which connects with the main Spanish (Renfe) train line from Barcelona. There are three stations above Ribes-Enllaç: Ribes-Vila, Queralbs, and Núria. On the first 3½ miles of the journey the *cremallera* functions as a standard railway train, but the cog railway comes into play as the incline increases. Package tickets are available that combine Renfe and the *cremallera*. For those traveling by car, there is ample parking at the Ribes-Enllaç station. (http://www.valldenuria.com/website_valldenuria/eng/index.asp)

The fortified bridge over the river Fluvià

Besalú, Garrotxa

What's this? Not another medieval town in Catalunya, complete with Jewish history and Romanesque churches? Indeed, yes! Another medieval town! And it's a wonderful one, resembling a miniature, just-discovered Girona: it has a river (in fact, several come together), a twelfth-century fortified bridge, recently excavated Jewish sites including a rare ritual bath, two Romanesque churches worthy of a visit, a hint of mystery—and far fewer tourists. (Elyn)

Besalú was the Roman town Bisuldunum, which means "a fortress between two rivers." In this case the two rivers are the Fluvià and the Capellades, the latter of which is nearly dry. The entrance to the older section of the town is via the fortified bridge, which dates from the eleventh century but has been rebuilt a number of times. Besalú was named a National Historical-Artistic Site in 1966 due to the state of conservation of its many historic buildings. Besalú, unlike Barcelona and Girona, is not yet a major tourist destination even though there are many treasures here. It is an evocative place, its narrow streets laden with ghosts and history.

The Call and *Mikveh*

The most powerful area in Besalú is the *mikveh* (also spelled *mikvah* and *miqva*) in the old Jewish quarter (Call), which was fortuitously discovered in the 1960s. A *mikveh* is a religious bathhouse used to regain purity after various events, such as contact with a dead body or eating the meat of an animal that died of natural causes, or after sexual activity or menstruation. Its construction must meet a number of requirements,

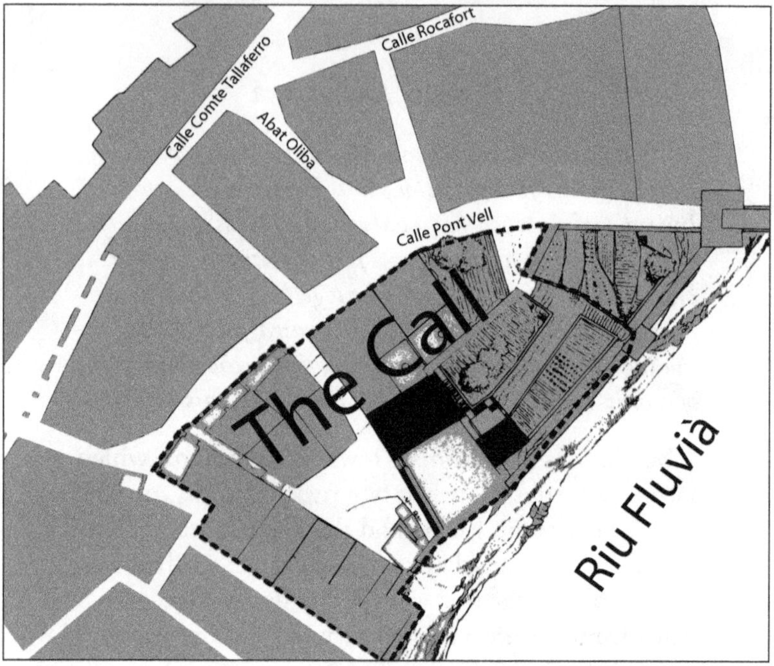

The Call

including access to a constant flow of fresh running water. Historically, the *mikveh* and the synagogue were the religious centers of the Jewish community. After the discovery of the mikveh in 1964 the search began for the synagogue. This bore fruit in 2003 with the discovery of the site of the synagogue, a school, and a *yeshiva* (a center for the study of classical Jewish texts). These areas are now clearly marked and there is an interpretive center on the site.

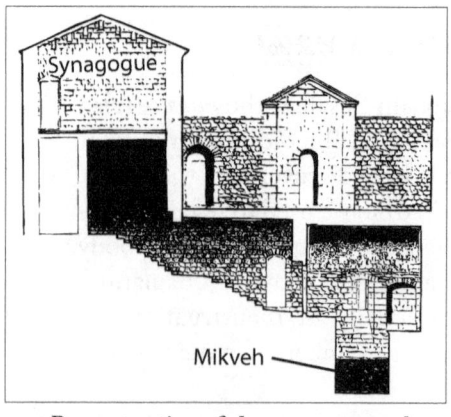

Reconstruction of the synagogue and mikveh

The mikveh

The *mikveh* was sealed off by the Jews when they left in 1415—perhaps hoping to return? It gradually silted in and the level of the river descended, depriving the *mikveh* of the required supply of moving water. Restoration work has freed the *mikveh* of silt, and city officials regularly keep some water in the pool to indicate its original purpose. This water is stagnant, so it no longer fulfills the basic requirement for a *mikveh*.

Elyn spent some time alone in the *mikveh* and reported that her impression was of deep sadness in the place. Its original purpose of purification was now completely defeated because it was filled with stagnant water. But it still is a powerful place and well worth a visit.

City officials have made a good attempt to bring the discovery of the Call and its restoration to the attention of tourists. There are interpretative centers that provide information and video presentations. Only the foundations of the synagogue, school, and *yeshiva* remain, but the *mikveh* more than makes up for that.

Església de Sant Pere

The Església de Sant Pere (Church of St. Peter) is all that remains of the Benedictine monastery that was founded in 977 by Count-Bishop Miró III Bonfill. The church building dates from the twelfth century, but some parts were constructed later. In particular, the bell tower is a seventeenth-century addition. The church is one of the most important Romanesque buildings in Catalunya and was an important pilgrimage shrine.

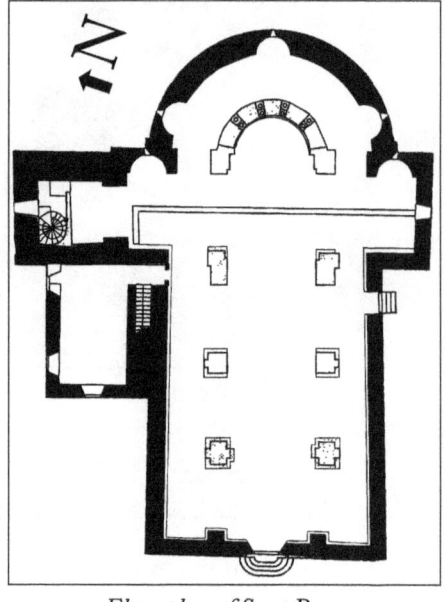

Floor plan of Sant Pere

The outside of the building makes it appear that there is only one apse, but when you enter you see that there are three apses built into the very thick outer walls of the ambulatory. The construction of an ambulatory behind the altar is characteristic of pilgrimage churches. Pilgrims could enter through the left nave and circumnavigate the church by the ambulatory, venerate the holy relics of St. Prius and St. Felician in the side chapels, and leave through the right nave without disturbing the service that might be in progress.

The lions on the façade

The front of the building is austere, with an undecorated western doorway and three small windows, one on the left and one on the right, and a larger window in the center high above the central nave. The decoration of the larger window is distinctive, with a lion on either side standing over a monkey on the left and a prone male figure on the right. According to the tourist office guide, the lions were protecting the church from evil forces such as man's animal nature (the monkey) and sins such as lust (the prone male figure is covering his sex). The lions are not very realistic because the sculptor had never seen the real animals. Elsewhere (at the Hospital de Sant Julià) our guide said the lions with one head and two bodies represented duality—the choice between good and evil. We concluded that lions could stand for many things.

We dowsed the interior of this church and found significant energy lines through the main nave, with other energy lines crossing near the pillars and at the altar. See what you feel.

Interior of Sant Pere, looking down the nave to the altar

Other Things to Do and See

Walking the streets of medieval Besalú is a powerful experience, effortlessly transporting you into the past. The town has a number of interesting sites. You can walk the curiously angled bridge, which has beautiful views back into the city. (The angle comes from the builders having chosen natural rock outcroppings as footings for the bridge.) St. Vincent Church (Sant Vicenç) has six nineteenth-century oil paintings that have been recently restored and are quite beautiful. It also has a well-guarded reliquary with a piece of the "true cross" that Catalan politician Francesc Cambo gave to the town in 1923 as a replacement for the earlier relic that was stolen in 1899.

Besalú is on the eastern edge of La Garrotxa (see pp. 58-67) and is a good entry point to the volcanic region. Traveling west about eight miles from Besalú, toward Olot, you will reach the town of Castellfollit de la Roca stunningly perched atop a spectacular cliff of columnar basalt. This is one of the more photographed sights in the Garrotxa region, and the town itself is worth a stop. Most of the buildings in the older section are of volcanic stone and the view from the old church is spectacular. Further west are Ripoll and Sant Joan de les Abadesses (see pp. 69-73). (http://www.besalu.cat/eng/)

Getting There

Besalú is easily reached by car from Figueres (21 miles) or Girona (20 miles). There is no train service to Besalú, but busses run from Figueres, Girona, or Olot (http://www.teisa-bus.com). Taking a train to Girona

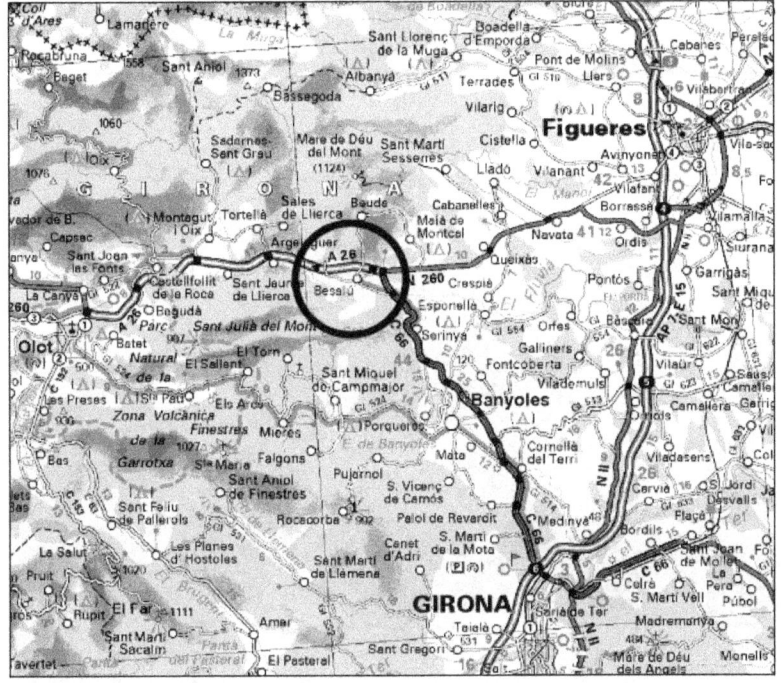

Area map

and renting a car there would be a good option. For those who enjoy hiking, the area has numerous trails that link major points. Purchase the Itinerànnia map and guidebook for the Garrotxa region from Editorial Alpina (http://www.itinerannia.net).

Notes

Dolmen Puig de Caneres

Dolmen Puig de Caneres, Darnius, Alt Empordà

Nestling in the middle of a field, the dolmen waits patiently for those who seek it out. Our companion, Anne, calls it the "love bug"—a fitting name for this small dolmen, the size of a large VW Beetle. I breathe and center myself. The dolmen does seem to radiate gentle, sweet energy. I stroke its capstone, puzzling at my gesture: after all, it's just a pile of ancient stones, not a living creature—isn't it?

We greet the dolmen, then meditate within its shelter and on its flat, warm capstone. We prepare to "activate" it, to rouse it from its slumber. As the energy levels rise, I feel disoriented, confused. I turn and flee into the nearby forest. I sit upon a lichen-covered rock and breathe the shady, leaf-filtered air. I feel more grounded here, surrounded by vibrant green. In the distance, undulating wave patterns radiate from the dolmen like heat waves rising from asphalt on a hot summer's day. (Elyn)

Dolmen Puig de Caneres, which dates from 3500 BCE, is a megalithic monument in an isolated field near the town of Darnius in Alt Empordà. The first published mention of the site was in 1893. In that publication Lluís Marià Vidal writes that the dolmen is in a field owned by the lords of Eras House, Mr. and Mrs. Puig.

The stones are granite with some black intrusions that may be hornblende. We have seen similar stones in megalithic sites in Scotland and Brittany (see *Powerful Places in Scotland,* Calanais I, p. 62), leading us to speculate about why the megalith builders seem to have preferred granite for their constructions. The presence of significant amounts of quartz in granite may have something to do with it. Quartz is known to develop an electrical (piezo-electric) charge when subjected to pressure. When you rub two pieces of quartz together, you can see a glow within caused by the distortion of the crystals.

The dolmen in 1912

Regardless of the scientific explanations, we often experience considerable energy associated with megalithic sites. Some of this may be due to the underground water and fault lines, some to the constructions themselves. To experience this for yourself we remind you of the BLESSING and ECOLOGY acronyms (pp. 9-11). Your approach to a powerful place will in large part determine your experience there, although some places are so powerful that they practically demand your attention.

> "We do not ourselves need to believe in the gods of our forebears to appreciate that they lived closer to the land and were more aware of it. By contrast, we find ourselves a bit embarrassed that today we can live surrounded by some of the forces they tamed, and yet be completely oblivious to them." John Burke and Kaj Halberg, *Seed of Knowledge Stone of Plenty*. San Francisco: Council Oak Books, 2005, p. 175.

Geomancers believe that dowsing and performing specific rituals can activate sacred sites such as dolmens and properly constructed churches. They call this "opening" the energy of a

Anne following a boundary

site. This book is not the place to attempt a complete explanation of this process, but we will suggest a few simple things you can try. Dolmen Puig de Caneres is a good place to start since it is isolated and in an open field.

If a dolmen has been "opened" recently you may be able to sense rings of energy around it at certain intervals. These concentric rings of energy are referred to as the harmonics of a place. The ring nearest the center is the first harmonic; they are numbered out-

---

"A dolmen marks a place where the energies of Heaven and Earth form a special link. The dolmen, like any other type of megalith or ancient temple, if built with appropriate measures, orientation, and correct placement, has the function of harmonizing an area by potentiating the union of cosmic-telluric energies. The result of that union is what we call 'creative energy.' It can be sensed like a dome that encircles and surrounds the dolmen.

"Depending on the characteristics of the site and the dolmen, this dome may vary in size. Sometimes it is many miles wide and tall. The dome of creative energy and the structure of the dolmen relate to the place, creating a structure of subtle bodies and gates.

"When we 'activate a dolmen,' we are awakening and potentiating, with our intention, that union of cosmic-telluric energies to generate new processes of information among all the parts—that is, to create patterns that allow for the manifestation of consciousness in its essence." Ferran Blasco private communication, January 3, 2010.

ward from there. Some people can sense this a long distance away.

Start at the beginning of the path and walk slowly toward the dolmen with arms at your sides and palms facing outward. Try to sense shifts in energy. These will feel like subtle boundaries. Some people describe them as places where the air feels thicker on the palms. Others may feel a slight tingling sensation. Some fortunate individuals are even able to see the energy enclosures. It is important to focus on "feeling" not "doing."

Gary meditating on the capstone

The rings may be almost circular in shape, with the dolmen at the center, or they may be more irregular. When you think you sense a boundary, try to follow it around the dolmen. If you are able to follow the boundary you may come to a "doorway," a place where there is an opening in the ring. If so, enter that doorway and search for another boundary. Continue searching, following boundaries, and entering doorways until you reach the dolmen. (This same process can be followed when you

> "Heightened radiation levels were also measured inside Neolithic and Iron Age stone chambers. This was because they are enclosed granite structures. ... Places of heightened background radiation may have been sought for healing purposes.... The Dragon Project became convinced that areas of heightened background radiation could also trigger visionary experience...." Paul Devereux. *Earth Mysteries.* Piatkus Publishers, 1999, pp. 52, 55.

> "Given what we now know about the capabilities of the chambers, we consider it likely that they were utilitarian structures, serving an eminently practical purpose—rather than being solely ritual or cultural—and that this was the cause of their almost worldwide distribution." John Burke and Kaj Halberg, *Seed of Knowledge Stone of Plenty*. San Francisco: Council Oak Books, 2005, p. 73.

approach certain trees—but that is another discussion.) Try meditating both inside and on top of the dolmen. Notice how different the two experiences feel.

There may be several rings of energy around a dolmen if it has been recently opened, or only one or two if it is "quiet." Detecting the energetic boundaries and following them will have some effect on the energy of the dolmen and may raise it. As a bonus for your work, remember that you have impacted the energy of the place, and any increase in energy makes a positive contribution to the place itself and those who come later. To fully open or activate a site requires several additional steps, which are too complex to describe here.

Where does the energy come from? From the construction itself and the location of the site. Usually a dolmen (or standing stone or stone circle) is located over underground energy lines. Also, the geometry (mea-

View of the dolmen from the forest

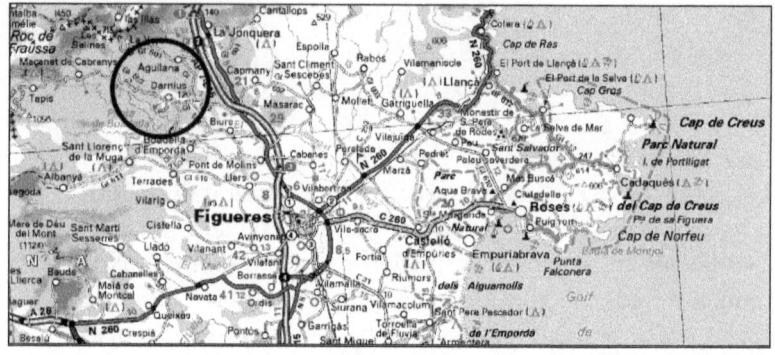
Area map

surements and shape) and astronomical alignment of a structure may follow certain principles that the builders knew.

What is the purpose of the energy? People have used the energy of sacred sites for healing, to increase the power of rituals they perform, and to enhance the fertility of the seeds they plant and the yield of nearby fields. In addition, there are probably other purposes that we don't know about.

When Anne and Gary "opened" Dolmen Puig de Caneres, Elyn found the energy so intense that she had to flee. Elyn's experience is an important reminder that not all energies are for everyone.

Other Things to Do and See

The northeast section of Catalunya is filled with ancient sites of all kinds. Roman and Greek sites abound and many have been restored. The Cap de Creus area has a number of important megalithic sites (see pp. 98-109). The coast at Cap de Creus has numerous resorts with extensive beaches. Nearby Figueres is famous for its Dalí Museum. Consult a general Spanish travel guide for details.

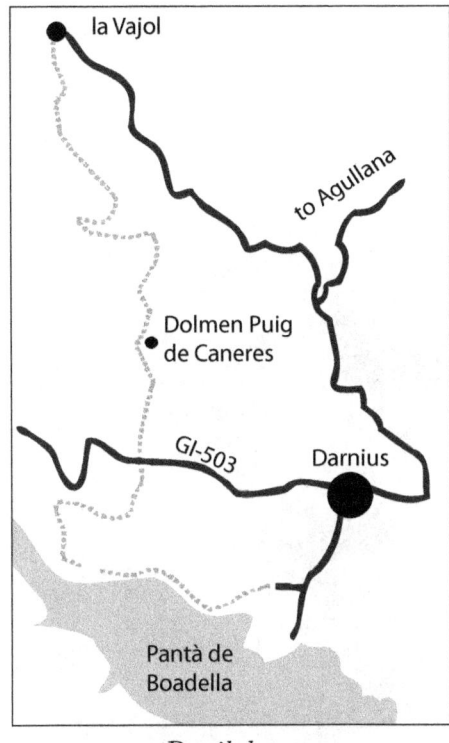

Detailed map

Getting There

Dolmen Puig de Caneres isn't marked on most maps. Drive west through Darnius on GI-503 and take the dirt road to the right after about 1.5 miles. This corner is marked with a road sign. Drive down the dirt road; after about a mile you will see the dolmen on the right. It is visible from the road, so keep driving until you actually see it. (There's a large boulder on the right beside a dirt road a short distance before you reach the dolmen. That's not it.)

Notes

Sant Pere de Rodes

Cap de Creus, Alt Empordà

Water on three sides, stupendous views: we follow the sinuous road that winds its way around the last spur of the Pyrenees as they reach the sea—the most eastern point of Iberia. Numerous dolmens dot the ridges, some in isolation, others clustering together. Why do they bunch together, overlooking the sea? The fortress-like ruined monastery of Sant Pere de Rodes stands sentinel on Verdera Mountain, built over the ruins of a Greek or Roman temple of Venus. A sacred spring still marks the spot. I climb a pitch-black staircase to St. Michael's chapel, high above the nave. Why Venus? Why St. Peter? Why St Michael? Why here? A crossroads and ancient holy place, the mountain vibrates with forgotten memories, with the elemental energies of water, fire, earth, and air.... (Elyn)

Cap de Creus is the easternmost edge of the Pyrenees, which sink abruptly into the Mediterranean. The contrast of mountain and sea is extreme, and it attracted the megalithic builders. They constructed numerous dolmens and erected many menhirs in a very condensed area. There must have been a powerful attraction to the location.

The view from Sant Pere de Rodes

The Pyrenees themselves have a fascinating creation story. At one time (150 million years ago) the entire landmass of what is now Spain and Portugal was a large island (or a mini-continent) in the Atlantic Ocean. Iberia (the name given to this mini-continent) moved slowly in a southeastern direction; around 80 million years ago it collided first with Africa and then with Europe. The point of impact with Africa was at Gibraltar (think of the Rock of Gibraltar); Iberia gradually turned, and the Pyrenees were formed when it smashed into Europe over the next 60 million years.

Dolmen del Puig Margall

Dolmen del Puig Margall

We begin our brief tour of the Cap de Creus by driving up the GIP-6041 from Vilajuïga. There is a group of at least ten dolmens, approximately 4,000 to 6,000 years old. Many of these structures were built to be seen from each other (see "intervisibility" on p. 4), but we can only speculate about why this was important to the megalith builders. They left few clues to help us solve the mystery.

After numerous twists and turns, you'll see a sign for the Dolmens de les

Dolmen de les Vinyes Mortes

View from Dolmen del Puig Margall. Dolmen de les Vinyes Mortes visible near the road

Vinyes Mortes on the right side of the road. The dolmen nearest to the road has been heavily reconstructed. You'll be able to see the Dolmen del Puig Margall from the road, higher up and on the left side of the hill.

Park the car nearby, walk up the road, and follow the brush-covered path on the left. Dolmen del Puig Margall has a pleasant, cozy feel, nestling in the bushes. Elyn said that it was friendly, like a puppy, as she gently stroked its capstone. The energy inside, however, is very strong, due to a crossing of energy lines near the back. We recommend meditating both inside and on the top of this dolmen; notice how you feel.

Anne inside Puig Margall

If you have a good hiking map you can find the remaining dolmens in this group. We recommend purchasing the *Mapa-Guia Excursionista* for *Cap de Creus Parc Natural (E-25)*, published by Editorial Alpina.

Monestir de Sant Pere de Rodes

Continuing on the GIP-6041 toward Port de la Selva you will come to the ruins of the Monestir de Sant Pere de Rodes. Founded in the eighth century, Sant Pere de Rodes was one of the most powerful Benedictine monasteries in Spain by the tenth century. It was also an important place of pilgrimage. The large complex is one of the most impressive Catalan Romanesque monuments. It is a UNESCO World Heritage Site.

Monestir de Sant Pere de Rodes

Legend has it that, in the seventh century, Pope Boniface IV sent the head of St. Peter, along with relics of some other saints, to Cap de Creus to protect them; he feared for their safety if the infidels invaded Rome. The relics were hidden in a grotto in the Sierra de Rodes. However, when the emissaries of the pope returned to find them, the grotto—and the relics—had vanished. The monastery was constructed on the site and dedicated to St. Peter.

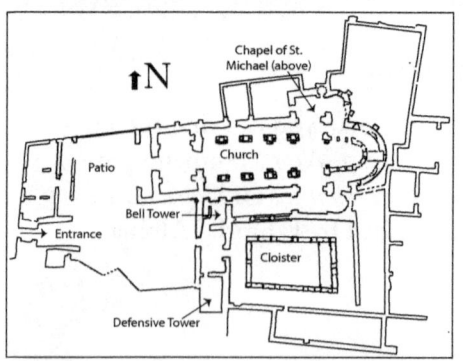
Floor plan of the Monestir de Sant Pere de Rodes

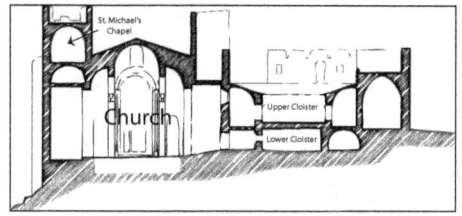

Sant Pere de Rodes elevation

Recent excavations suggest that the monastery was built over a temple to Venus Pirene (note similarity between the goddess's name and the Pyrenees). Nearby Empúries was an important Greek port by 600 BCE; Romans invaded the peninsula some 400 years later, so it would not be surprising that there was a pagan temple on the mountaintop. Some capitals in the monastery were, indeed, carved from the remains of Greek or Roman marble.

To the north, nestled in the hillside just below the monastery, is a pretty grotto with a fountain. Some experts believe this was originally a fountain dedicated to Venus and consider it further evidence of pagan antecedents. See what you experience when you go there: can you feel the faint resonance of the goddess?

In a tower on the north side of the church is the small Chapel of St. Michael (Capella de Sant Miquel). This seems to us to be additional confirmation of the presence of an ancient temple

The Venus or Monks' Fountain

because chapels to St. Michael were often constructed over pagan shrines.

St. Michael is shown in armor on horseback with a long lance subduing a dragon. One interpretation is that the dragon represents the power of

> "The early Christian Church went as far as to issue directives that, in every case possible, new churches should be sited on old pagan 'power spots.' This, of course, was considered desirable for three reasons: the priestly geometricians of the church would harness the power, worshippers of the old religions would continue to come to the site, and the original pagan artifacts would be destroyed." Stephen Skinner. *Sacred Geometry – Deciphering the Code*. New York: Sterling, 2009 (paperback), p. 11.

the older earth-based religions (or the underground energy lines) and St. Michael's role is to subdue—but not extinguish—these forces. The interior spiral staircase inside the tower is normally kept locked but you may be able to get a guide to open it for you. It's quite an experience to climb in the darkness! The chapel can also be reached via an external staircase from the nave. The Chapel of St. Michael was used for ceremonies restricted to only the monks. It has a very special "feel."

There are those who feel that the restoration of Sant Pere de Rodes has been far too extensive and that it was a more powerful site when it was a ruin. We don't share that view, but it is something you might consider. Try to experience the power of this place, perched high on the mountainside, the sea far below. Imagine watching the

> "These sites need to be approached with a mind that is not the ordinary mind. It's not about 'doing' but about what you bring to the site. That is what determines the results." Ferran Blasco, private communication.

sunrise from here, long before the sun's rays have reached lower ground.

The view of the coast from Sant Pere de Rodes is spectacular and not to be missed. If you want a particularly exciting ride, take the GIP-6041 down to the Port de la Selva. It is an exposed mountain road with several switch-backs.

The Dolmen Route from Roses

Just outside of the resort town of Roses on the south coast of Cap de Creus is a well-marked trail that takes you to nearly a dozen dolmens and menhirs. In Roses, drive to the corner of Gran Via Pau Casals and Carretera a Montjoi. A small sign points toward the "Dolmen Route" in the direction of Montjoi. Do not assume that other streets will connect with the road to Montjoi—they don't. (We made that mistake and found ourselves driving up a vertiginous road to the top of Puig Rom.)

Dolmen La Creu d'en Cobertella

A half-mile outside of Roses on the Carretera a Montjoi you will come to a sign that reads "Dolmen Creu de la Creu d'en Cobertella." The entire trail takes about one hour and 15 minutes to walk. The trailhead is well marked on the left and there is parking at the site. A short (three-minute) walk up the trail brings you to the largest dolmen in Catalunya, La Creu d'en Cobertella, which dates from the third millennium BCE. It is a beautifully preserved megalith made with exceptionally large stones. The dolmen is encircled with low steel fencing (to protect it or to protect visitors?), but there is evidence that people have climbed over.

Dolmen La Creu d'en Cobertella from the front

Elyn felt that this dolmen was like a "wise elder"—very ancient and filled with wisdom, but not a site to be taken lightly. The dolmen has an outer passageway formed by two very large, flat stones, leading to a doorway into an inner chamber. The entryway faces south. We found the energy at the doorway to be very strong. It seemed to

> "Almost all ancient peoples created their temples and other sacred spaces with careful reference to the correct numbers, geometry and proportion. Geometry governed the very movement of the heavenly bodies and the seasons. The megalithic builders of Britain and the designers of the pyramids in Egypt applied this sacred geometry to the positioning and orientation of their constructions." Stephen Skinner. *Sacred Geometry – Deciphering the Code.* New York: Sterling, 2009 (paperback), p. 6.

Anne at Menhir Casa Cremada II

us to be a warning to "keep out."

Continuing up the trail you come to the Menhir Casa Cremada II, which faces almost due south and north. This standing stone was knocked down sometime in the early twentieth century, but it has been carefully restored to its original position. You can see evidence of restoration near the base, but the restoration was carefully done and the energy of the stone feels intact. We have heard that single standing stones often mark the crossings of energy lines and Casa Cremada II is no exception. We quickly found the energy lines (a water line and a dry fault) and they cross precisely at the menhir. See if you can feel the underground lines.

Continuing up the trail you can enjoy breathtaking views of the Gulf of Roses and surroundings. There are at least six more dolmens and menhirs that you can easily reach before the trail circles around through an olive grove and vineyards and brings you back to the parking area.

Other Things to Do and See

There is much more to see at Monestir de Sant Pere de Rodes than we have described, including a two-level cloister, a tenth- to eleventh-century crypt, and towers. Nearby are a pre-Romanesque church (Santa Creu de Rodes) and the remains of a medieval village and castle (Sant Salvador de Verdera). Down the hill from the monastery you will find the charming fishing village of Port de la Selva. The Museu d'Història de Catalunya website has much additional information that is useful (http://www.en.mhcat.net). An interesting and very detailed history of the Port de la Selva area can be found at http://www.crae.com/pap/MostrarP.asp?Idp=38&Idi=3. There are websites that mention other dolmens in the area. The following is a good one: http://www.cbrava.com/dolmen/dolmen_uk.htm.

The seaside resort town of Roses offers beaches, shops, and excellent restaurants as well as access to the "Dolmen Route." A few miles inland is Figueres, with the Dalí museum.

Getting There

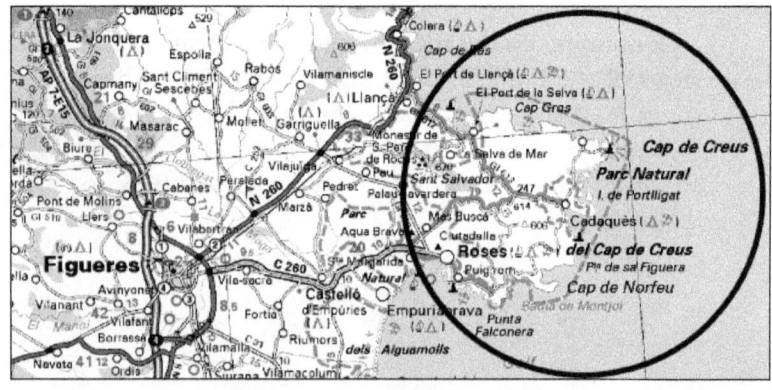

Area map

To see the places we have described you will need a car and good hiking shoes. Public transportation is available to the resort town of Roses, but the dolmens, menhirs, and Sant Pere de Rodes are only reachable by car or by hiking. One way to reach Cap de Creus is: from Figueres, take N260 in the direction of Llançà. Turn off onto GI-610 to Vilajuïga. There, follow the GIP-6041 up the mountain to the dolmens and Sant Pere de Rodes (and over to Port de la Selva, if you desire). Excellent and well-marked hiking trails crisscross the entire Cap de Creus area. Whether you choose to explore by car or on foot, we highly recommend the very detailed map and guidebook, *Mapa-Guia Excursionista* for *Cap de Creus Parc Natural (E-25)*, published by Editorial Alpina (www.editorialalpina.com or www.geoestel.com).

Notes

Afterword

We hope you have enjoyed learning about these powerful places in Catalunya and will experience some of them on foot, by cog rail, or by car. They vary greatly—bustling cities, enchanted forests, medieval villages, mountain sanctuaries, and ancient megalithics—but they are all, in their different ways, powerful places. It is our intention in this series to show you how to "be" in a powerful place—not merely visit it. We hope we have succeeded.

Catalunya is a large autonomous community, filled with numerous powerful places. We have focused on sites that are clustered in the north and along the northeast coast. You'll be surprised at how close they are to each other. The roads are good and the infrastructure solid.

We have found the Catalans to be proud of their rich heritage (they just celebrated 650 years of Catalan government) and eager to share it with interested visitors. Don't hesitate to seek beneath the surface, to spend an extra day or two exploring a particularly intriguing site. If you're like us, you'll want to return again and again. There is much more to see!

Glossary

apse A curved area at the end of a church, often the location of the altar.

archetype The original pattern or model from which all things of the same kind are copied or on which they are based.

basilica An early Christian or medieval church of the type built especially in Italy, characterized by a plan including a nave, two or four side aisles, a semicircular apse, a narthex, and often other features.

BCE Before the Common Era (contemporary replacement for BC, which stands for Before Christ).

Black Madonna or **Black Virgin** A statue or painting of Mary in which she is depicted with dark or black skin, especially referring to those of the medieval period or earlier. Often associated with healing miracles.

blind spring Underground water feature that has not broken through to the surface.

boss An ornamental, knoblike projection, such as a carved keystone at the intersection of arches in the vaulted ceiling of a church.

Bronze Age An age that began with metalworking, specifically the smelting of copper and tin to make bronze. The Spanish Bronze Age is from 2200-750 BCE. Associated with various types of cairns, sometimes built inside Neolithic henges or tombs.

cairn A man-made pile of stones, often in a conical form. They may be of recent construction or very old. Also refers to a megalithic tomb covered with small stones. Those we describe were constructed in Neolithic times.

Call The Catalan name for the Jewish section of a town.

capital The top part of a pillar or column, often carved.

castells The human tower popular in Catalunya, made up of tiers of people *(castellers)* standing on each other's shoulders.

CE Common Era (modern replacement for AD, which stands for Anno Domini—in the year of the Lord).

Celt A nineteenth-century term used to describe any of the European peoples who spoke, or speak, a Celtic language. The term is also used in a wider sense to describe the modern descendants of those peoples, notably those who participate in a Celtic culture. A member of a group of Indo-Europeans found in Germany and France in the 2nd Millennium BCE, and in Spain by the 6th century BCE.

cloister A covered walk, especially in a religious institution, having an open arcade or colonnade usually opening onto a courtyard.

crypt A subterranean chamber or vault, especially one beneath the main floor of a church.

dolmen A type of single-chamber megalithic (large stone) construction, usually consisting of three or more upright stones supporting a large flat horizontal capstone. Most date from the early Neolithic period (4000-3000 BCE). Although often used for burials, they were also ceremonial or "power" centers. They were initially covered with earth or small stones to form a barrow or tumulus, but in many cases that covering has weathered away.

dowse To search for underground supplies of water, metal, etc., by the use of a divining rod or pendulum.

duende A fairy- or goblin-like creature in Spanish and Latin American folklore.

fada Catalan word for a "fairy." In Spanish, *hada*.

follet Catalan word for "elf."

Franco, Francisco (1892-1975) Dictator of Spain from 1936 until his death in 1975.

hermitage A place where one can live in seclusion; a retreat; a kind of small church.

intervisibility Visible to each other. Megalithic sites were often constructed to be within sight of each other.

Kabbalah A body of mystical teachings of Jewish origin, often based on an esoteric interpretation of the Hebrew Scriptures. Also spelled Qabalah or Cabalah.

megalith A large stone which has been used to construct a structure or monument, either alone or together with other stones. Megalithic means structures made of such large stones, utilizing an interlocking system without the use of mortar or cement. They date from 4500-1500 BCE in Europe.

menhir An upright monumental stone standing either alone or with others, as in an alignment.

mikveh A ritual bath to which Orthodox Jews are traditionally required to go on certain occasions, e.g., the Sabbath and after each menstrual period, to cleanse and purify themselves.

modernista A decorative style in Spanish art, architecture, and literature from about 1890 till World War I. The Catalan interpretation of Art Nouveau.

nave The central part of a church, extending from the narthex to the apse and flanked by aisles.

Neolithic The New Stone Age. A period in the development of human technology, beginning about 9500 BCE in the Middle East (6000 BCE in Spain), that is traditionally considered the last part of the Stone Age. The Neolithic people were farmers who domesticated plants and animals and created pottery and woven textiles. They built numerous constructions, including dolmens, stone circles, and earthen henges and erected many standing stones. The period ends when metal tools became widespread in the Copper Age or Bronze Age or it developed directly into the Iron Age, depending on geographical region.

Republican In Spain, refers to those who, in the 19th and early 20th centuries, favored a republican form of government. They fought against the Nationalists during the Spanish Civil War (1936-1939). Franco's Nationalists won. The reprisals were brutal.

retablo An altarpiece in a church.

Romanesque A style of European church architecture containing both Roman and Byzantine elements, prevalent especially in the 11th and 12th centuries and characterized by massive walls, round arches, and relatively simple ornamentation.

sardana A dance of the region of Catalunya, Spain, in which the dancers form a moving circle.

Sheela-na-gig Figurative carvings of (often skeletal) naked women displaying exaggerated genitalia. They are found on churches, castles, and other buildings, particularly in the British Isles, dating approximately from the 11th to 16th centuries.

tau cross A cross in the form of a T. Also called the cross of Saint Anthony or St. Francis. Also symbol of Roman god Mithras, Greek Attis, and Tammuz, the Sumerian solar god.

"thin place" A place (in nature or in a human construction) where the veil between this world and other realms (fairy, the Other World, etc.) is thin and passage between our normal consensual reality and a different kind of reality is more easily accomplished.

telluric Of or pertaining to the earth; terrestrial. Telluric currents are underground energy lines.

tumulus A mound of earth and stones raised over a dolmen. Often referred to as a tomb, but served as more than a burial site. Tumuli are also known as barrows, burial mounds, *Hügelgrab* or *kurgans*, and can be found throughout much of the world.

vortex A funnel shape created by a whirling fluid or by the motion of spiraling energy. In dowsing, a vortex is spiraling subtle energy.

wouivre An old Gaulish name given to snakes that glide, to rivers that snake through the landscape, to telluric currents that snake underground from the depths of the terrestrial strata, bringing life that fructifies Earth and Man.

Bibliography

(This list includes books cited in this guidebook as well as books of interest)

Aviva, Elyn. *The Journey: A Novel of Pilgrimage and Spiritual Quest.* Santa Fe: Pilgrims Process, Inc., 2004.

———. *Walking Through Cancer: A Pilgrimage of Gratitude on the Way of St. James.* Santa Fe: Pilgrims Process, Inc., 2009.

Begg, Ean. *The Cult of the Black Virgin.* Revised and expanded edition. London: Arkana – Penguin Books, 1996.

Boix, Maur M. *What is Montserrat.* Montserrat: Publicacions de l'Abadia de Montserrat, 1998.

Burke, John, and Kaj Halberg. Seed of Knowledge, *Stone of Plenty: Understanding the Lost Technology of the Ancient Megalith-Builders.* San Francisco: Council Oak Books, 2005.

Chaplin, Patrice. *City of Secrets.* Wheaton, IL: Quest Books, 2008.

Devereux, Paul. *Earth Mysteries.* London: Judy Piatkus (Publishers) Ltd, 1999.

——— *The Sacred Place: The Ancient Origin of Holy and Mystical Sites.* London: Cassel & Co., 2000.

Ferguson, George. *Signs & Symbols in Christian Art.* London: Oxford University Press, paperback edition, 1961.

Fox, Matthew. "The Return of the Black Madonna: A Sign of Our Times..." In *The Moonlit Path: Reflections on the Dark Feminine,* ed. by Fred Gustafson. Berwick, ME: Nicolas-Hays Inc., 2003.

Furlong, David. *Working with Earth Energies: How to Tap into the Healing Powers of the Natural World.* London: Judy Piatkus (Publishers) Ltd., 2003.

Goering, Joseph. *The Virgin and the Grail – Origins of a Legend.* New Haven: Yale University Press, 2005.

Kelly, Eamonn P. *Sheela-na-Gigs: Origins and Functions.* Country House, Dublin, in association with the National Museum of Ireland, 1996.

Lonegren, Sig. *Spiritual Dowsing.* Glastonbury: Gothic Image Publications, 1996.

Petzold, Andreas. *Romanesque Art.* Upper Saddle River, NJ: Prentice Hall, 1995.

Pogacnik, Marko. *Sacred Geography: Geomancy: Co-Creating the Earth Cosmos.* Great Barrington, MA: Lindisfarne Books, 2007.

Ramírez Muro, Verónica and Rocio Sierra Carbonell. *Secret Barcelona.* Versailles, France: Jonglez Publishing, 2008.

Schneider, Michael S. *A Beginner's Guide to Constructing the Universe – The Mathematical Archetypes of Nature, Art, and Science.* New York: HarperPerennial paperback edition, 1995.

Skinner, Stephen. *Sacred Geometry – Deciphering the Code.* New York: Sterling Publishing Co., 2006 (2009, paperback edition).

Sobrequés I Callicó, Jaume. *History of Catalonia.* Barcelona: Editorial Base, 2007, English edition.

Soler i Canals, Fr Josep. *All Montserrat.* Editorial Fisa Escudo de Oro, s/d.

Wallace-Murphy, Tim. *Cracking the Symbol Code: Revealing the Secret Heretical Messages within Church and Renaissance Art.* London: Watkins Publishing, 2005.

Weir, Anthony and James Jerman. *Images of Lust – Sexual Carvings on Medieval Churches.* London: B. T. Batsford Ltd, paperback edition 1993.

www.ingramcontent.com/pod-product-compliance
Lightning Source LLC
Chambersburg PA
CBHW031403040426
42444CB00005B/400